YOUR INVITATION TO SCRIPTURE

Your Invitation to Scripture

An Introduction to the Bible for Catholics

KEVIN PERROTTA

CHARIS

SERVANT PUBLICATIONS
ANN ARBOR, MICHIGAN

Charis Books is an imprint of Servant Publications especially designed to serve
Roman Catholics.

Servant Publications—Mission Statement
We are dedicated to publishing books that spread the gospel of Jesus
Christ, help Christians to live in accordance with that gospel, promote
renewal in the church, and bear witness to Christian unity.

All Scripture quotations, unless otherwise indicated, are from the New Revised
Standard Version of the Bible, copyrighted 1989 by the Division of Christian
Education of the National Council of Churches of Christ in the USA. Used by per-
mission. All rights reserved. Scripture verses marked RSV are from the Revised
Standard Version of the Bible.

NIHIL OBSTAT: Monsignor Robert D. Lunsford
                Chancellor
IMPRIMATUR: Most Reverend Carl. F. Mengeling
                Bishop of Lansing
                February 24, 2003

The NIHIL OBSTAT and IMPRIMATUR are declarations that a book or pamphlet
is considered to be free from doctrinal or moral error. It is not implied that those who
have granted the NIHIL OBSTAT and IMPRIMATUR agree with the contents, opinions, or statements expressed.

First published in 2000 by Charis Books, Servant Publications, as *Your One-Stop Guide
to the Bible*. This revised and expanded edition published by:
Servant Publications
P.O. Box 8617
Ann Arbor, MI 48107
www.servantpub.com

Cover design: Brian Fowler. Grand Rapids, Mich.

03 04 05 06 10 9 8 7 6 5 4 3 2 1
Printed in the United States of America

ISBN 1-56955-343-2

Library of Congress Cataloging-in-Publication Data

Perrotta, Kevin.
  Your Invitation to Scripture : an introduction to the Bible for Catholics /
Kevin Perrotta.
     p. cm.
Includes bibliographical references (p.   ) and index.
  ISBN 1-56955-343-2
1. Bible--Introductions. 2. Catholic Church--Doctrines. I. Title.
BS475.3.P44 2003
220.6'1'08822--dc21

                                                          2003004802

Contents

Preface

If you know anything at all about the Bible, you know that writing a complete two-hundred-page guide to the Bible is as impossible as mapping the human genome on a postcard. The Bible is just a *little* too big and too deep for a single book to supply all the help a new reader needs! What is possible, though, is a short book to get you started reading the Bible—a book that gives you a basic orientation to what the Bible is, how to make sense of it, and how to read it as God's word to you. That is the purpose of this book.

Realistically, there is no way to talk about the Bible without introducing a few names and dates, facts and figures, technical terms, and even a word or two of Hebrew and Greek. But I have kept the details to a minimum. At the beginning of your discovery of the Bible, it is more important to get the big picture than to absorb a lot of data. A good study Bible—an edition of the Bible with explanatory articles and plentiful notes—will provide you with a wealth of details. I urge you to get one (see chapter nine). The present book will help you see why you would want to know all the information a study Bible contains.

The Bible is both simple and complex. Because it is simple, you can start reading it without special preparation. Yet as soon as you begin to read, you meet questions too big for ten-second explanations.

Consequently, even an introductory book must deal with some difficult subjects. I have tried to write as simply as possible. But given the complexity of some of the issues, a few of the chapters have a steep learning curve. If you find a chapter heavy going (I'm thinking particularly of chapter seven on interpretation), you might prefer to skim it at first and return to it later on.

If you know anything about the study of the Bible, you know that scholarly debates swirl around virtually every line. I could have introduced many statements in this book with the qualification, "in the view of many scholars..." After many statements, I could have added, "although not all experts would agree." Rather than cluttering up the book that way, it seems simpler just to tell you here that I have necessarily made choices between various scholarly opinions. Not everyone with expertise in the Bible would agree with my every statement (or with each other's). I have, however, stayed within the mainstream of current biblical scholarship.

In addition, throughout the book, I have attempted to convey an understanding of the Catholic approach to Scripture. I hope that all my explanations are in harmony with the Church's teaching.

If you are completely new to Bible reading, you may find it helpful to read the section on finding your way around in the Bible (pages 142–44) before you begin.

Well, now, onward into the Bible. Let us be guided in our exploration of the sacred text by the advice of St. Augustine: "Let us pray, so that we might understand."

Chapter One

What Have We Here?
The Bible at First Glance

When you pick up a Bible, you hold more than a book. You have a library in your hands. The word *Bible* comes from the Greek language. In ancient Greek, *biblíon* meant a book written on a scroll; the plural, *ta biblía,* meant "the books," that is, a library.

It is fitting that this particular library should have a Greek name, for a good deal of it was written in Greek. An even larger portion, however, was written in Hebrew. A few sections were written in a sister-language to Hebrew called Aramaic. So what most of us hold in our hands is a translation—a point we will consider more fully in chapter nine.

The Bible is less like the public library down the street than like a collection of books in a home. The books in my house reflect our family's tastes and background. In a similar way, the Bible reflects the tastes and background, the needs and interests of the people of God in centuries past. Why they chose these particular books to be in their library, while leaving similar works out, is a point we will consider in chapter six.

Every library has some kind of order to it. As we will see in the next chapter, the Bible has a rather careful and significant arrangement. As any library, the Bible contains books written at various times by various authors. The books are also of different types. While some of the biblical books testify to historical events, history is not the only kind of writing found in the library. Among the biblical books are a collection of prayers (Psalms), reflections on life (Proverbs and other books), personal letters (for example, Philemon), and much more. There is even a small shelf of fiction containing short stories, one of which is pretty funny (Jonah).

While the library analogy is helpful, it takes us only so far. For the Bible is different from any library in an important way: It has a beginning and an end. Thus the Bible is not only a *collection* of books; it is a *book*, in which all the parts are related to each other.

The Bible has two main parts. The first, longer part begins with accounts of the creation of the world, then focuses on the fortunes of a small, ancient Near Eastern people called Israel. This first part traces the Israelites' ups and downs over more than a thousand years, ending about a century before Jesus of Nazareth.

The second part begins with accounts of Jesus. After a narrative about his followers, the second part continues with a collection of early Christian letters. It concludes with a book that offers a symbolic vision of history, the end of the world, and a new creation.

In Christian tradition, the two main parts of the Bible have been called *testaments*. Testament in this sense is an obsolete word for "compact" or "covenant," a solemn agreement binding parties together. The term is used in reference to the Bible because each of the Bible's two main parts is organized around a covenant.

The first part, which Christians call the *Old Testament*, revolves around the covenant God made with the people Israel through their leader Moses. The second part, called the *New Testament*, focuses on the covenant God has made with the entire human race through Jesus Christ. The testament terminology points to the Bible's main subject: the deep, enduring relationship that God has entered into with us, his human creatures.

The Bible, Christians, and Jews

The collection of books that Catholics call the Old Testament includes the books that constitute the Bible for Jews. Catholics should be aware, however, that Jews do not call their Scriptures the *Old* Testament, since they do not regard this collection of books as a prelude to any further testament. Some Jews, in fact, find the term "Old Testament" offensive, because calling God's covenant with Israel "old" seems to imply that it has come to an end and has been replaced by a new covenant through Jesus. The Catholic Church does not, in fact, believe that the covenant between God and Israel has been terminated. For this reason, when speaking with Jews, many Catholics avoid referring to the biblical books that Jews and Christians have in common as the Old Testament.

Among Christians, a popular substitute for "Old Testament" is the term *Hebrew Scriptures* (with a corresponding term—*Christian Scriptures*—for the New Testament). The term "Hebrew Scriptures" is not offensive to Jews, and it has been used in discussions with Jews by Pope John Paul II. It has the disadvantage, however, of seeming to imply that this portion of the Bible belongs only to Judaism and not to Christianity also. A further consideration is that "Hebrew Scriptures" does not accurately describe the contents of the Catholic Old Testament, since some of Catholics' Old Testament books are not contained in the Jewish Bible, and these additional books are not in Hebrew, but in Greek (see pages 14 and 22–23, 38).

One alternative for Catholics in discussion with Jews is simply to use the term *Scripture* for both the Old Testament and the Jewish Bible. Another option is for Catholics to refer to the Old and New Testaments as the *First Testament* and the *Second Testament.* Or they may use the less formal terms that Pope John Paul II employed when speaking with Jewish leaders in Mainz, Germany, in 1980: "the first and the second parts of the Bible."

A further approach is for Catholics both to keep their traditional terms and to learn a new one. Thus, first, in speaking with Jews, Catholics may continue to use the term Old Testament, with the explanation that by calling it "old" we do not mean obsolete or abolished. Old is good! We apply it to the first part of the Bible as an expression of respect.

Second, we could learn to use the term that Jews themselves use for their biblical collection: *Tanakh* (see pages 22–23). *Tanakh* (rhymes with "a knack") expresses respect for the Jewish Bible and avoids confusion and misunderstanding. And it is not difficult to say.

It is worth noting that in 1999 the American Catholic bishops affirmed that the terms "Old Testament" and "New Testament" belong to the "language of faith" and should be used by Catholics at least in materials for religious education.

Chapter Two

What's the Message?
Getting the Bible's Big Picture

If the Bible is a library of ancient books, why read it? Lots of ancient texts, pressed onto clay tablets or scratched onto sheets of papyrus, are lying around in museums. We leave them to specialists. What is so different about the biblical books that they deserve our attention even if we are not terribly interested in ancient history and literature? The answer lies in the Bible's message, a message that is as important today as it was when it was written, thousands of years ago.

To grasp the Bible's message, a good place to begin is the table of contents. The Bible tells a story. The arrangement of the parts points us toward the story line and thus toward the central message. We have already seen that the Bible is divided into the Old and New Testaments. If you look more closely, you will notice that within each testament the books are grouped in sections according to types.

The Old Testament

Historical Books
In the Old Testament, the first grouping is a set of *historical books.* The placement of historical books at the beginning of the Bible tells us something right away: The Bible speaks about history. It is concerned with events in the real world, not simply with ideas.

True, the Bible also contains poems, visions, legends, and other non-historical material. And, true, the biblical authors employed symbolic

OLD TESTAMENT

Historical Books
The Pentateuch
Genesis
Exodus
Leviticus
Numbers
Deuteronomy

Other Historical Works
Joshua
Judges
Ruth
1 and 2 Samuel
1 and 2 Kings
1 and 2 Chronicles
Ezra
Nehemiah
Tobit
Judith
Esther
1 and 2 Maccabees

Reflective or Prayerful Books
Job
Psalms
Proverbs
Ecclesiastes
Song of Songs
Wisdom
Sirach

Prophetic Books
The Major Prophets
Isaiah
Jeremiah
Lamentations
Baruch
Ezekiel
Daniel

The Minor Prophets
Hosea
Joel
Amos
Obadiah
Jonah
Micah
Nahum
Habakkuk
Zephaniah
Haggai
Zechariah
Malachi

Note: Some of the Old Testament books recognized by the Catholic Church are not recognized by Protestants and are not part of the Bible recognized by Protestants and Judaism. These are Tobit, Judith, 1 and 2 Maccabees, Wisdom, Sirach, Baruch, and parts of Daniel and Esther. Catholics call these the "deuterocanonical" (that is, "second" portion) works; others refer to them as the "apocrypha" (literally "hidden" works, here meaning inauthentic). See pages 85–87.

NEW TESTAMENT

Historical Narratives
Gospels
Matthew
Mark
Luke
John

A History of the Early Church
Acts of the Apostles

Correspondence
Letters Associated With Paul
Romans
1 and 2 Corinthians
Galatians
Ephesians
Philippians
Colossians
1 and 2 Thessalonians
1 and 2 Timothy
Titus
Philemon
Hebrews

Letters Associated With Other Figures
James
1 and 2 Peter
1, 2, and 3 John
Jude

A Prophetic Vision
Revelation

language to speak about God (for example, God led the Israelites out of Egypt "by a mighty hand and an outstretched arm"—Deuteronomy 4:34) because there is no way to avoid metaphors and analogies when speaking of the Creator. Nevertheless, the Bible is historical in its bones. It testifies to God's activity in our real-time world.

Like all generalizations about the Bible, the classification "historical book" needs to be qualified. To be precise, the historical section of the Bible contains some short fictional works (Tobit, Judith, and Esther: see pages 36 and 58). And the historical section leads off with some chapters that are neither history nor fiction in a modern sense. The first book of the Bible, Genesis (the Greek word for *origin*), begins with eleven chapters that recount God's creation of the world and other prehistoric events. Here we find Adam and Eve, Cain and Abel, Noah and the flood, and the Tower of Babel. To some extent these accounts draw on ancient legends and mythical materials in order to communicate fundamental truths about God and the human race (see pages 52–54).

B.C. and A.D.

B.C. stands for "Before Christ," A.D. for "*Anno Domini,*" which is Latin for "In the Year of the Lord." Both designations are traditional in Western culture. A common alternative in discussions involving non-Christians is the abbreviations B.C.E. and C.E., which stand for "Before the Common Era" and "Common Era." The American Catholic bishops regard B.C. and A.D. as part of the "language of faith" and urge Catholics to continue to use these abbreviations in religious education.

While these early chapters are not exactly history, they provide the background for the history that the biblical writings go on to narrate. These "prehistoric" stories show that God created the earth to be home for a race of creatures with whom he wished to have a deep, lasting relationship—the human race (Genesis 1–2). These early chapters also show that humans did not wholeheartedly embrace God's purposes. By turning away from God, we brought conflict, suffering, even death, on ourselves (Genesis 3–11).

After the first eleven chapters of Genesis, the historical books go on to show that God did not give up on our race but put into effect a plan for restoring us to himself. In pursuit of this plan, God gathered and guided the people called Israel. Among the people of Israel, God began to restore the wholeness, peace, and closeness to him that he wished the human race to enjoy from the beginning.

God launches this plan by calling a shepherding couple, Abraham and Sarah, and promising them and their descendants protection, offspring, and land (Genesis 12–50). The next book, Exodus (Greek for *going out*), tells of God's bringing their descendants out of slavery in Egypt probably around the year 1250 B.C. through the leadership of a man named Moses and making a covenant with them in the desert of Sinai (Exodus 1—18). God then instructs them in the way he wishes them to live (Exodus 19–40, Leviticus, Numbers). Before he dies, Moses urges the Israelites to be faithful to God's instructions (Deuteronomy). These first five books of the Bible, called the *Pentateuch* (see page 19), establish the basis for God's dealings with Israel as a people.

At the end of the Pentateuch, the reader may wonder how the Israelites responded to God's call. The rest of the historical books provide the answer:

- The Israelites settle in Canaan and the territory to the east—roughly modern Israel, Palestine, and western Jordan (around 1200 B.C.; the Book of Joshua).
- They live as a tribal confederation (roughly 1200 to 1020 B.C.; the Book of Judges).
- They enjoy a brief moment in the sun as a powerful nation under kings David and Solomon (1000 to 922 B.C.; 1 and 2 Samuel; 1 Kings 1–11; 1 Chronicles 11–2 Chronicles 9).
- They endure the breakup of their nation into a northern and a southern kingdom (called respectively "Israel" and "Judah"). A process of decline and defeat leads eventually to the destruction of both kingdoms, with the deportation of the leading members of the southern kingdom to Babylon—present-day Iraq (587 B.C.; the rest of the Books of Kings and Chronicles).

In the historical books, God expresses his desire for his people to be fully devoted to him and to show justice and kindness toward one another. This involved their staying clear of the many gods their neighbors venerated, some of whom functioned as icons of militarism, economic oppression, and sexual immorality.

Yet God's longing for the Israelites to be faithful to him repeatedly met with a disappointing response. The Israelites showed an inclination to worship other gods, to mistreat each other, and to ignore God's warnings, turning to God only in moments of crisis. That is to say, they behaved just as we might expect any group of human beings to behave. The historical books thus contain a lasting reminder of the moral flaws we all share.

God showed himself to be patient to the Israelites, yet unwilling to allow their infidelity and injustices to go unchecked indefinitely. Finally, he let them be overwhelmed by their enemies.

Scrolls

The biblical books were originally written on papyrus scrolls rather than on pages bound between covers. The practice of writing on scrolls is reflected in the name sometimes given to the first five books of the Bible, *Pentateuch,* which is Greek for "five cases for holding scrolls."

Beyond a certain length, a scroll became unwieldy. Compositions that extended beyond that length might be divided into two scrolls. Three of the historical books of the Old Testament were long enough to require two scrolls each. Thus we have 1 and 2 Samuel, 1 and 2 Kings, and 1 and 2 Chronicles. The separation of these histories into two parts, which originated because of the requirements of scroll-writing, continues today in our printed Bibles, even though the division is no longer necessary.

Note, however, that the historical books of 1 and 2 Maccabees do not follow this pattern. They are distinct works, not part one and part two of a single book. Similarly, the numbered letters in the New Testament (1 and 2 Corinthians, 1 and 2 Thessalonians, 1 and 2 Timothy, 1 and 2 Peter, and 1, 2, and 3 John) are separate works.

As Jerusalem burned and the Israelites of the southern kingdom were dragged off into captivity in Babylon (the end of 2 Kings and 2 Chronicles), the story of God and Israel launched in the Pentateuch seemed to have ended in failure. But some fifty years later, God opened the way for some of the exiles to return to Jerusalem. They went home determined not to repeat their ancestors' mistakes. Thus the historical writings resume and show us:

- The return of exiles from Babylon under Persian emperors; their restoration of the Jerusalem temple and, on a small scale, of their community life (beginning about 539 B.C.; the Books of Ezra and Nehemiah).

- Their struggles against Greek-speaking emperors in Syria (beginning around 175 B.C.; the Books of the Maccabees).

From the whole sequence of the historical books, a portrait of God emerges. He is kind, generous, loyal, deeply concerned about justice among people, forgiving, reluctant to discipline yet insistent that people respond to his love. Because God repeatedly shows compassion and mercy to his people, a pattern of rescue and blessing emerges in his dealings with them. Thus, his action on their behalf in one age becomes the model for his later actions. God's leading his people out of slavery in Egypt sets the precedent for his leading them out of Babylon (Isaiah 43:14-21).

At the conclusion of the historical books, Israel has not found lasting peace and wholeness. Yet God's actions in history have given grounds for confidence that he has something better in mind. The God of a good creation, the merciful God of the exodus from Egypt, the God of covenant faithfulness toward Israel in exile—how could *this* God settle for anything less than his people's complete freedom from every evil? By attesting to God's compassion and loyalty across centuries, the historical books nourish the hope that he will continue to act in the future.

Reflective or Prayerful Books

The second Old Testament grouping consists of *reflective* or *prayerful books*. These books do not chart a forward movement of God's plans on the stage of world history but rather exhibit a deepening of his presence in his people's minds and hearts. Here we find personal prayers and community hymns (Psalms), folk wisdom and the pondering of values (Proverbs), discussions of individual and social life (Job, Ecclesiastes, Wisdom, Sirach), even love poetry (the Song of Songs). In these writings the people of Israel meditated on God's saving deeds, his covenant, and the way of life he had given them, and they spoke to God in appeals, complaints, thanksgiving, and praise.

Prophetic Books

The third Old Testament grouping—*prophetic books*—resumes the focus on God's involvement in world events. These books preserve the messages of men whom God authorized to speak for him in the period covered by the historical books.

Again, as with the grouping of historical books, a qualification must be made. This grouping is only *broadly* prophetic. One work of historical fiction (about the real-life prophet Jonah) has found its way into this group, and a couple of nonprophetic books (Lamentations and Baruch) are shelved here because of their traditional association with the prophet Jeremiah.

The prophets did not preach general truths. Their message was not merely "justice is good, oppression is bad." They delivered God's analysis of the actual people and institutions of their day. In the prophets' words, God communicated his view of how well his people were conducting the political, economic, religious, and personal aspects of their life. Through the prophets, God injected his judgment-bringing and life-sustaining word into particular historical situations (1 Kings 17:1-7; Jeremiah 23:29).

For the most part, the prophets seem to have communicated God's purposes for their own present and near future, without envisaging distant ages to come. But the divine promises they conveyed were not entirely fulfilled in their own times. The prophet who delivered the messages of Isaiah 40–55, for example, predicted that the exiles in Babylon would make a glorious return to their own land. But the actual events fell short of the predicted glory. In fact, the predictions

---

The Books of the Jewish Bible: *Tanakh*

Torah **("Instruction" or "Law")**
    Genesis
    Exodus
    Leviticus
    Numbers
    Deuteronomy

Nevi'im **("Prophets")**
   The Former Prophets
    Joshua
    Judges
    1 and 2 Samuel
    1 and 2 Kings

   The Latter Prophets
    The Major Prophets
     Isaiah
     Jeremiah
     Ezechiel

    The Twelve
     Hosea
     Joel
     Amos
     Obadiah
     Jonah
     Micah
     Nahum
     Habakkuk
     Zephaniah
     Haggai
     Zechariah
     Malachi

Ketuvim **("Writings")**
    Psalms
    Proverbs
    Job
    Song of Songs
    Ruth
    Lamentations
    Ecclesiastes
    Esther
    Daniel
    Ezra
    Nehemiah
    1 and 2 Chronicles

The Jewish Bible is called *Tanakh,* an acronym for *T*orah, *N*evi'im, *K*etuvim. All the books of *Tanakh* are contained in the Catholic Old Testament, but *Tanakh* is shorter than the Catholic Old Testament (compare the listing here with that on page 14, and see also pages 11–12). Also, the books are arranged in different orders in the Jewish and Catholic biblical collections.

In the Jewish Bible, the first five books constitute a section, called the *Torah,* meaning "instruction" or "law." Marked off as a distinctive unit, these five books form the foundation of Jewish belief and practice. The second section, called the *Prophets,* contains not only the writings of prophets but also historical narratives (called the *Former Prophets*). The third section, the *Writings,* overlaps the section of reflective and prayerful books in the Catholic Old Testament, but it includes also historical narratives and a prophetic book (Daniel).

The sequence of Torah—Prophets—Writings—gives the Jewish collection a different focus from the Christian Old Testament. In *Tanakh,* the *Torah* is the center of attention. The Prophets and the Writings follow it in roughly descending order of importance. Because the less weighty writings are placed at the end of the collection, the reader's attention is directed back to the beginning of God's dealings with Israel. By contrast, in the Catholic Bible the prophetic books' position at the end of the Old Testament gives the Old Testament an orientation to the future, looking forward to an action of God that has not yet occurred.

received only token fulfillment (compare the grand expectations of Isaiah 60–62 and Ezekiel 36:22-38; 40:1–43:12 with the modest fulfillment reflected in Ezra 3–4, 9; Nehemiah 1–6; and Haggai 1).

The prophets looked forward to God's acting on a global, even cosmic scale, and at a profound depth within men and women, bringing about a condition of profound peace, well-being, and holiness. They promised that God would reconcile his people to himself (Isaiah 44:21-23), heal them of their tendency to resist him (Jeremiah 31: 31-34), renew the earth (Isaiah 65:17-25), remove injustice (Isaiah 59:15-20), gather his scattered people (Isaiah 60; Zechariah 10:6-12), overcome their enemies (Isaiah 49:22-26), and dwell splendidly in their midst (Isaiah 52:7-12; 54:4-8). In sum, the prophets looked for God to achieve his original intentions for humankind. By the end of the period of Old Testament prophecy in the second century before Christ (the Book of Daniel), these promises hung in the air, awaiting a humanly incomprehensible fulfillment.

Thus a surplus of expectation in the prophets' words was carried forward to a later time. The prophetic books, even more than the historical books, give rise to the expectation that God has great things in store for Israel and the world. The Church highlights this forward thrust in the prophetic writings by placing them at the end of the Old Testament. So the Old Testament concludes on a note of expectancy (Malachi 4), peering into the future to see what God will yet do.

The New Testament

Narratives

As the Old Testament begins with a historical section, so also does the New. Among the *narratives* of the New Testament, the *Gospels* ("announcements of good news") come first. They convey the news of the life, death, and resurrection of Jesus of Nazareth. The Gospels' placement immediately after the Old Testament signals that they communicate the fulfillment of the expectations that God aroused through his saving actions and prophetic words in the history of Israel.

In the Gospels, God attains in a preliminary way the purpose he had pursued since his creation of the human race. God opens up a deep, lasting relationship with the human race by entering into our human world as one of us. The process of God's revelation of himself to Israel reaches its climax in his appearance among us as the human individual, Jesus of Nazareth. All of God's previous words to the human race culminate in this taking-flesh of the divine Word (John 1:1-14).

The patterns of God's merciful dealings with Israel achieve their fullest expression in Jesus. In Jesus, God accomplishes the decisive exodus, from the slavery of sin and death into moral freedom and eternal life. In Jesus, God brings about his people's decisive return from exile—the human race's return home from the estrangement of sin into eternal life with him. Through Jesus, God grants men and women a new, deeper covenant with himself, a covenant by which the Spirit of God lives in human hearts.

Jesus claimed to enjoy a unique relationship with God and thus to stand at the apex of God's dealings with Israel (John 5:19-47). With his own appearance on the scene, Jesus announced, the arrival of God's kingdom had become imminent (Mark 1:14-15). Jesus pointed to himself as the one who would fulfill God's promises to free the people of Israel from their enemies, to grant them forgiveness, to gather them together, to establish his presence among them.

But Jesus fulfilled Israel's God-given expectations in a radically unexpected way. He set himself to defeat not the Roman occupiers but deeper enemies: human sinfulness, the devil, and death. He conquered not by military might but by self-sacrificing love, allowing himself to be nailed to a cross. He restored God's people not, as some of his fellow Jews might have expected, through a more exact observance of the details of the Mosaic law, but by gathering disciples, laying down his life for them, and giving them the Holy Spirit.

Jesus did not accomplish the Jewish national renewal and repossession of the ancestral homeland that some longed for. Instead, he inaugurated a renewal for all men and women. In this way, Jesus fulfilled the global purposes for which God had chosen the people of Israel in the first place.

By grouping the Gospels together at the beginning of the New Testament, the Church expressed the priority of Jesus. This point emerges clearly from the placement of the Gospel of Luke and the Acts of the Apostles. These two books were written by Luke as a two-volume work. Yet the two parts are separated in order to put Luke's Gospel with the other three Gospels in lead position. The Gospels first! Jesus first!

In one sense, with the Gospels, the forward thrust of God's actions and promises reaches its goal. The arrow hits the target. Yet the Gospels too point forward. God's action through Jesus now extends outward from first-century Palestine to embrace men and women everywhere until the end of time. Each Gospel ends with Jesus' assurance of his continued presence with his followers as they go out to offer all men and women—us!—the invitation to join his community and experience life in his Spirit.

Jesus' fulfillment of God's purposes is definitive but not yet fully manifest. Forgiveness, the gift of the Spirit, empowerment for personal and social transformation—these aspects of God's kingdom are now present. But there remains a more comprehensive coming of the kingdom, when God will cleanse creation of evil and unite men and women with himself forever, raising us up through resurrection to live as new creatures in a new creation. Jesus' resurrection is the beginning of this new creation. The completion is yet to come.

The Gospels, then, are not the end of the Bible, but its watershed. The Old Testament books track God's actions leading up to Jesus' coming. The rest of the New Testament books enlarge on its meaning and implications.

Shelved immediately after the Gospels is the Acts of the Apostles—volume two of Luke's narrative work. In this history of the beginnings of the Church, Luke shows how the news of Jesus began to spread throughout the world. Acts breaks off without a neat conclusion. By its incompleteness, the ending looks toward the future—to us, who are invited to enter into this unfinished history and help to complete it.

Correspondence
Just as the narrative books of the Old Testament are followed by reflections and prayers, the narrative books of the New Testament are followed by reflections (with prayers) concerning who Jesus is, what he has accomplished, and how we should respond to him. The content of these writings is not academic-style theology. These are letters from pastoral leaders—Paul, James, Peter, John, Jude, and perhaps some of their followers—to communities of Christians struggling to understand Jesus and follow him in their particular circumstances. They are down-to-earth communications about the life and mission of Christ's first-century followers. These letters continue to speak to us in our very different situations.

A forward-looking orientation runs through the New Testament letters. From beginning to end, this early Christian correspondence is marked by the expectation of Jesus' glorious return to complete the coming of God's kingdom.

A Vision

The Old Testament ends with prophetic works that look forward to God's future activity. The New Testament ends with a single prophetic work—the Book of Revelation (or the *Apocalypse*, from the Greek word for "an unveiling" or "a revealing"). This visionary work is the climax of prophecy. In symbolic language it portrays Jesus' death and resurrection as the culmination of God's action in the world and shows the impact of that event on all of history between Jesus' resurrection and his return. This final New Testament book, and thus the Bible as a whole, concludes with its gaze directed toward the future, awaiting God's fulfillment of his plans for the human race.

Thus the total arrangement of the biblical books from Genesis to Revelation expresses the course of God's interactions with the human race from creation to new creation. The ordering of the biblical books displays the working out of a single, overarching, divine plan—God's plan to give his life to the human race, a plan of faithful, patient love. We who read the Bible in the twenty-first century are invited to participate in the final stage of God's activity in history—the stage that began when Jesus rose from the dead and will continue until he returns. We cannot know how long this stage will last. Nevertheless, we are called to prepare for its conclusion, when God will bring to perfection his reign over all that he has created.

Chapter Three

How Did It Come to Be?
The Formation of the Bible

Most of us do not spend much time wondering how the books we read were put together. We are usually less interested in the authors' labors than in the results. Why should it be any different when it comes to the Bible? The reason is that in the case of the Bible, understanding the process is useful for understanding the outcome.

A modern book is typically produced by someone who can read and write. An individual author (possibly a team of authors) composes the manuscript in a fairly short period, usually less than a year. Customarily the author is identified by name. Although an editor makes changes, the book emerges from the press as an expression of the author's views. There is a strong interest in presenting something new—new information, new ideas, new approaches.

Sprinkle the words "not" and "not necessarily" throughout the preceding paragraph, and you will begin to get an idea of how the Bible was produced. That is to say:

- Some of the material in the Bible probably originated with people who did not read or write, for example, the families of Abraham, Isaac, and Jacob. Some of it comes from literate people who preferred to express themselves orally, for example, Samuel and Jesus.

- Although some biblical books are the work of individual writers (the prophecy of Micah, Paul's letter to the Galatians), many reflect the efforts of multiple contributors (Exodus, Proverbs).

The contributors did not all necessarily work as a team; they may have lived in different places, even in different centuries (Genesis, Isaiah).

- A succession of people added to and reshaped the texts, blurring the distinction between writing and editing (Deuteronomy, perhaps John). These texts reflect not just the views of an individual but of a community.

- More often than not it is impossible to determine who the writers and editors were (Chronicles, Hebrews) or even when they lived (Ruth, Psalms). Authors may have deliberately hidden their identities because they were not seeking to promote their individual views but to hand on the traditions of their community.

- The authors and editors enlarged or revised the oral and written traditions they received, so that the traditions might speak afresh to their own times. Nevertheless, their intention was not to offer anything innovative but rather to pass on faithfully what they had received (see, for example, Luke 1:1-4; 1 Corinthians 11:23-26; 15:1-7; 1 John 1:1-4).

Few of the books in the biblical library are books in the modern sense—writings that an individual composed in his or her own name, expressing his or her individual views. While many distinctive voices make themselves heard in the Bible, to some degree all the biblical books are the crystallizations of traditions. The Bible is the written form of the traditions of ancient Israel and the early Church.

From Oral Traditions to Finished Product

The neatness of the Bible's table of contents contrasts with the sometimes untidy processes by which the book reached its final form. To bring these processes into view, let us take a quick walk through several historical periods to observe the Bible under construction. The point of this brief tour is not to investigate exactly when and how each of the biblical books was composed (in many cases, these questions are the subjects of complicated scholarly debates), but simply to get a feel for the length and complexity of the process. The rounded dates are approximations.

Undetermined Centuries Before 1250 B.C.

God spoke to the ancestors of Israel—Abraham, Sarah, and others—promising them the blessings of offspring and land. They wrote nothing. For unknown numbers of generations, their descendants handed on traditions about these patriarchs and matriarchs by word of mouth.

1250 to 1200 B.C.: Exodus From Egypt, Covenant at Sinai, Settlement in Canaan

The Israelites added their recollections of these great events to their growing stock of community lore. They may have written down short accounts in poetry or prose, but for the most part they probably continued to pass on their traditions in spoken form.

1200 to 1000 B.C.: Tribal Confederation

Tales of God's action through leaders such as Deborah and Samson were added to the community's oral traditions (Judges 4–5; 13–16). A few of God's instructions for their way of life were put in writing by the prophet Samuel (1 Samuel 10:25). But Samuel himself carried on a spoken ministry and left no written collection of prophecies.

1000 to 922 B.C.: Beginnings of the Monarchy

Only now, centuries after the exodus from Egypt, did the process of committing oral traditions to papyrus get seriously underway. The royal court of David and Solomon, and the temple that Solomon built, provided educated men with the setting and resources for the task. What some scholars call the "primary history" of Israel—the great national history running from Genesis through 2 Kings—probably began to take shape as men transposed oral traditions into texts. Even so, the written output in this period may have been meager. In any case, the writing and rewriting, adding and subtracting, editing and rearranging of historical material that began in this period was to continue for centuries.

Although in this period various authors and editors may have worked on the narrative and legal material that eventually evolved into the Pentateuch, these first five books of the Bible became associated with Moses, since he had played the central role in leading the people from Egypt and mediating God's covenant to them in the Sinai desert. In time, these books came to be called "the Books of Moses" and were thought to have flowed from his pen.

For generations before the monarchy, priests and people had been singing prayers at regional shrines. Now some leaders, probably at the temple in Jerusalem, began to gather these prayer songs, or "psalms." The collection became associated with David, possibly because he gave an initial impetus to the project. Exactly how the Book of Psalms (the "Psalter") developed is a matter of much scholarly discussion. But it certainly grew incrementally over centuries. Even by Jesus' day, a millennium after David, the collection had not quite reached its final form, as can be seen in first-century scrolls found near the Dead Sea, in which the exact number and order of the psalms varies slightly from one copy to another.

Also during the period of Solomon, learned people in Jerusalem began to collect wise sayings. Probably over a period of centuries, this collection evolved into the Book of Proverbs. The collection came to be associated with its early patron, Solomon, as did some later "wisdom" books (Ecclesiastes, Wisdom, Song of Songs).

922 to 721 B.C.: From the Dividing of the Kingdom to the Fall of the Northern Kingdom

Drawing on oral traditions, religious leaders in the northern kingdom of Israel, and perhaps also in the southern kingdom of Judah, wrote portions of the book we now call Deuteronomy (possibly chapters 5–11, 28). These writings, which took shape more than three centuries after Moses' death, contain instructions that he laid out on behalf of God for his people.

At the same time, new material was entering the community's tradition in oral form, in the prophecies of men such as Amos, Hosea, and Micah. Although their disciples preserved their words in writing, the prophets themselves continued to exercise mainly oral ministries. This is evident in accounts of two especially notable prophets, Elijah and Elisha, who did not leave behind any written works of their own (1 Kings 17–19, 21; 2 Kings 1–2, 4–8, 13).

721 to 587 B.C.: From the Fall of the Northern Kingdom to the Fall of the Southern Kingdom

At some unknown time, the portion of Deuteronomy written before 721 B.C. had been filed away and forgotten. Its later unexpected discovery in Jerusalem caused a great deal of public soul-searching (2 Kings 22:3-20). This may have been the first time in Israelite history that God's word in *written* form played a decisive role in events. The draft of Deuteronomy confronted Israel with a stark choice between obedience to God, leading to blessing, or disobedience to God, leading to destruction.

The outlook of Deuteronomy seems to have made an impact on the authors who were then at work on the "primary history" of Israel. Deuteronomy inspired them to highlight the dynamics of faithfulness-leading-to-blessing and unfaithfulness-leading-to-destruction in the history of Israel's relationship with God. Because of this influence of Deuteronomy on the ancient historians, modern scholars refer to the historical books from Joshua to 2 Kings as the "deuteronomist" history.

Despite this compositional activity, the spoken word continued to be the preeminent vehicle of God's communication with the people of Israel. In oral proclamation, prophets brought God's word to bear on the declining fortunes of the southern kingdom, although their prophecies were soon written down (Isaiah of Jerusalem—Isaiah 1–39; the prophet Jeremiah).

587 to 539 B.C.: Exile in Babylon
The conquered Israelites' period of suffering far from home bore fruit in a profound revitalization of their relationship with God. Prophecies delivered by Ezekiel and by an anonymous prophet whose words were added to those of Isaiah (Isaiah 40–55) spurred repentance and hope among the exiles.

More than *seven centuries* after the exodus from Egypt, authors and editors working during the exile brought the Pentateuch close to completion. Perhaps at this stage, while the Israelite authors were living in Mesopotamia, they added the accounts of creation and the primeval stories at the beginning of Genesis (Genesis 1–11). In composing these prehistoric accounts, they seem to have drawn on material that belonged to the general cultural heritage of Mesopotamia.

The biblical authors may also have refashioned the patriarchal narratives (Genesis 12–50) in such a way as to give the exiles in Babylon confidence that God's promises of land and blessing to their ancestors would yet be fulfilled in their own lives. The authors revised the laws of the Pentateuch to make a workable constitution for their renewed community, if and when they were allowed to return to their homeland. With a chastened view of Israel's failure to heed God's word, editors completed the historical books from Joshua to 2 Kings, bringing out the lessons to be learned from the moral and spiritual failures of the past.

539 to 333 B.C.: Reestablishment in the Land of Israel Under Persian Rule

In all the literary activity mentioned above we can see the increasing emphasis that the Israelites were placing on God's word in written form. But after the exile in Babylon, the prophets Haggai and Malachi communicated God's word in spoken form.

In this period, a prophet or prophets whose names are unknown spoke words of encouragement that were preserved at the end of the book of Isaiah (Isaiah 56–66). Thus the book of Isaiah contains a tradition spanning some two hundred years, from the mid-eighth to the mid-sixth centuries.

Leaders of the returning exiles composed accounts of contemporary events (the Books of Ezra and Nehemiah). In Nehemiah we read of a significant occasion on which God's written word played a key role in events, when Ezra's reading aloud to the people from the Pentateuch brought them to the point of tears (Nehemiah 8). The same circle of religious leaders produced a revised history of the preexilic period (1 and 2 Chronicles) designed to steer the community toward trust in God and a life centered on worship in the temple.

333 to 100 B.C.: Greek-Speaking Emperors, Jewish Revolt, and Autonomy

This period spans roughly the time between the conquest of Alexander the Great and the arrival of the Romans in Palestine. Sometime during these years, two authors produced works that probed the unpredictability and injustices of life (Ecclesiastes, Job). These authors used traditional proverbs and wise sayings to produce critiques of traditional views.

As pagan Greek culture spread throughout the Near East, other Jewish authors drew from Israelite traditions to reassure their readers that the God of Israel and his law, not the religious culture of Greece or Egypt, was the basis of a truly successful life (Wisdom, Sirach). Using background and characters from oral traditions, other authors wrote stories that gave beleaguered Jews courage and hope and provided examples of upright living (Esther, Judith, Tobit).

When Greek-speaking emperors in Syria began to persecute the Jews, devout persons elaborated on legends about a wise man named Daniel, supplementing these stories with prophetic visions to strengthen the Jews' faithfulness to God. The result was the Book of Daniel. The successful Jewish revolt, launched at about this time, was recorded in two somewhat parallel accounts (1 and 2 Maccabees).

5 B.C. to A.D. 30: The Life, Death, and Resurrection of Jesus of Nazareth

It is a fact of immense significance that Jesus, the central actor in the entire sweep of biblical events, did not leave any writings. He communicated his message entirely through spoken words and actions. Jesus drew men and women around himself so that they could observe his preaching and healings, his manner of life, his death and resurrection. He left the writing entirely to them.

A.D. 30 to 66: From Jesus' Ascension to the Death of the Apostles Peter and Paul

This was a phase of both oral and written communication about Jesus. After Jesus' death and resurrection, his followers focused not on writing about him but on making him known through preaching and personal contact. Thus the reports of Jesus' life and message passed through a short but crucial period of oral tradition. During this period, which lasted for some three or four decades, the apostles constantly shaped their reminiscences of Jesus to serve the purpose of helping men and women believe in him and follow him.

At the same time, it may well be that some Christians began to put Jesus' words and deeds into writing. As early as the first decade after Jesus' ascension, it seems, a written collection of his sayings began to develop. Many scholars refer to this no-longer-extant document as *Q*—from the German word *Quelle,* meaning "source." Some scholars think there was also a draft of some narrative material about Jesus written in Aramaic that was later enlarged into Matthew's or Mark's Gospel.

Meanwhile, Paul and other Christian leaders wrote letters to communities and individuals. Often these writers made references to the gospel preaching that had already become traditional in the early Church (1 Corinthians 2:1-5; 11:23-26; Galatians 1:6-9; 2:1-2; 1 Thessalonians 1:4-5; Titus 1:9). They incorporated material from the Christian communities' oral traditions: hymns (Philemon 2:6-11), confessions of faith (1 Corinthians 15:3-7), baptismal sermons (1 Peter 1), and moral instruction (1 Thessalonians 4:1-8).

A.D. 66 to the End of the First Century

Finally, the apostolic traditions about Jesus were put into definite written form. The recollections of Jesus by his first followers had been sharpened by their use in preaching and enriched by reflection. Now, with the help of early written documents such as *Q,* several authors composed narratives of Jesus' public activity, death, and resurrection. These are the written Gospels. They are the early Church's preaching about Jesus in written form.

It seems that associates of Peter and Paul applied these apostles' teaching to new circumstances a generation or so after their deaths (2 Peter, 1 and 2 Timothy, Titus). These letters were further crystallizations of the apostolic traditions.

In the closing years of the first century, a visionary named John wrote a vivid, symbolic portrayal of the conflict between the kingdom of God and the forces of evil during the period from Jesus' resurrection until his return (the Book of Revelation). This book draws together numerous historical and prophetic traditions in the Bible to show that God will ultimately fulfill his purposes for the human race through Jesus Christ.

What Languages Was the Bible Written In?

The Old Testament was composed in Hebrew, with a few exceptions. Part of Ezra, the book of Tobit, and part of Daniel were written in Aramaic. Judith, parts of Esther, the books of 2 Maccabees and Wisdom, and other parts of Daniel were written in Greek.

Some books were written in Hebrew or Aramaic but are preserved today only in Greek: parts of Tobit, the books of 1 Maccabees and Baruch, and parts of Sirach. The New Testament was written entirely in Greek.

Spoken Words

One feature that stands out in this brief survey is the large part played by the *spoken* word. In many cases, the word of God was in people's mouths long before they put it onto papyrus or parchment. Narratives, laws, prayers, poems, proverbs, prophecies—a great deal originated in oral form.

In the Old Testament period, even as some parts of the oral tradition were being set in writing (for example, the histories), new sources of oral tradition were opening up (for example, the prophets). By the time of Jesus, the Old Testament books were written, but with his appearance a new wave of oral material arose—his preaching, the apostles' preaching about him, early Christian hymns, creeds, and instructions.

The oral nature of the traditions preserved in the Bible gives them a particular character. Unlike written material, oral reports tend to be adjusted for each particular audience. Each time a speaker presents his or her material, he or she tries to highlight its relevance to the listeners by selecting, emphasizing, simplifying, rearranging, dramatizing, explaining. The speaker's goal is always to say something that is of immediate importance to the listeners. Everything outside that focus tends to drop away.

This tendency is easily seen in stories preserved by families. In my family's "oral tradition," for example, there is a recollection of why my grandfather left southern Italy to come to the United States. But this tradition does not include information that is not directly part of the story of my grandfather, for example, background explanations about the social and political situations in Italy or America at that time.

The fact that much of the Bible originated in spoken words does not mean that its historical narratives are unreliable. Ancient cultures placed a high value on the past. Traditions were carefully guarded. Memorization was more highly developed than in modern, literate societies. It was possible for accounts to be passed on intact over long periods of time. Nevertheless, material that is transmitted orally changes in ways that written traditions do not.

Oral traditions have a tendency to develop different versions. This seems to have occurred with some of the material that was eventually woven into the Bible. At various points, the biblical authors who put oral traditions into written form appear to have had available more than one rendition of a particular incident, prayer, proverb, or other material. The evidence for this multiplicity is that in some cases the authors seem to have woven more than one strand of oral material into their finished product.

For example, the authors of Genesis seem to have incorporated several traditions of God's promises to Abraham and Sarah (Genesis 12, 15, 17–18). By placing these variant oral traditions in a kind of sequence, they created a story that stretches over a period of decades. Thus the story dramatizes God's call to the couple to believe his promises and to await their fulfillment, even though for a long time it seemed unlikely. Despite the authors' masterful work, the finished product contains odd repetitions and apparent inconsistencies as the marks of its complicated history.

Authors Unknown

Our rapid survey of the Bible's development also highlights the fact that we must leave behind our modern concept of authorship when we open the Bible. We simply do not know the identity of most of the biblical authors. The names of Moses, David, Solomon, and Isaiah became associated with Old Testament collections of material that continued to grow long after their deaths. In the New Testament, Matthew's association with the first Gospel, Paul's with the "pastoral epistles" (1 and 2 Timothy and Titus), and Peter's with 2 Peter may be similar instances of the connecting of later material with earlier authoritative figures.

The attribution of later texts to earlier figures was in keeping with ancient convention. In biblical times it was acceptable to place new writings under the names of persons of the past.

The fact that we do not follow such a convention today does not diminish the value of the biblical writings. It is not necessary for the first five books of the Bible to have been written by Moses in order for them to express God's revelation. Challenges to the traditional attributions and speculation about the actual authorship of the biblical writings does not by itself call into question their status as inspired writings. Regardless of authorship, they authentically convey the traditions of Israel and the early Church. Indeed, it was precisely in order to *affirm* this authenticity that the ancient authors and editors masked their own identity and placed their works under the names of great personages of the tradition such as Moses and Solomon.

Rewriting and Editing

Writing gave oral traditions a more stable form. Yet even after being written down, the biblical writings belonged not to a university archive but to a community of people who enjoyed an ongoing relationship with a God who continued to unfold further stages of his plan for them.

In the Old Testament period, God led the people of Israel to a progressively deeper understanding of himself. As they experienced God's saving help and faithfulness, his correction and discipline, they grew in awe, love, and devotion. As they grew, they rewrote and edited the texts they had received from earlier generations. As the people of Israel saw new depths of meaning in past events, they revised their historical writings to clarify and express their insights. They adjusted old instructions to apply to new situations. In the writing of the Old Testament there were many scribes such as Jesus described, who knew how to bring out of their treasure what was old and what was new (Matthew 13:52).

The biblical authors venerated the traditions they received. Thus, when they saw a need for change, they often preferred to modify what they had received rather than eliminating it. In their writing and editing, there was an interplay between careful preservation and flexibility.

Thus an earlier view expressed in absolute terms in one text might be qualified by adding another view, sometimes right alongside the first. As a result, the library of the Old Testament contains both older and newer views of events and different perspectives on various issues. For example, the editors of 1 Samuel retained conflicting views about whether God wanted Israel to adopt a monarchical form of government (1 Samuel 10–11).

Another example is the biblical teaching about divine reward and retribution. The view of God's judgment emphasized in the books stretching from Deuteronomy to 2 Kings is expressed by Moses in his final sermon to the people of Israel: "If you obey the commandments of the Lord your God ... by loving the Lord your God, walking in his ways, and observing his commandments ... then you shall live and become numerous, and the Lord your God will bless you in the land.... But if your heart turns away and you do not hear ... you shall perish; you shall not live long in the land" (Deuteronomy 30:16-18).

This view, however, is subjected to a critique in Job and Ecclesiastes. These books point out that leading a virtuous life is no guarantee of receiving God's blessings. Bound together in the Bible, the contrasting perspectives modify each other. The assertion stands that God *does* make his judgments felt in this world (the view of the books from Deuteronomy to Kings). But this assertion is qualified by the rejoinder that God does not *always* execute judgment in this world (the contention of Job and Ecclesiastes). Rather than canceling each other out, the various writings together create a balanced view, showing that the truth is complex.

The process of reinterpretation and reapplication can be seen in every type of writing in the Bible. Here are a few more examples:

The patriarchal stories (Genesis 12–50), in which God makes promises to Abraham, Isaac, and Jacob, carried somewhat different messages to successive generations living in different circumstances:

- Before they went into Egypt, the descendants of the patriarchs were traveling shepherds living in small family groups. The stories of God's dealing with their ancestors Abraham, Isaac, and Jacob assured these vulnerable people that God had placed them under his protection.

- Later, during the tribal period in Canaan, these stories of the patriarchs reminded the tribes, who were living in different regions, that all who regarded Abraham, Isaac, and Jacob as ancestors shared a common call from God—and thus shared a commitment to defend each other.

- Later still, for the Israelites exiled in Babylon, God's promises of the land of Canaan to their ancestors nourished their hope that, even though their own generation had broken the covenant with

God, God, in his unconditional love and faithfulness, would nevertheless care for them and restore them to the land.

All these different levels of meaning may be detected in the finished form of Genesis.

Legal material in the Pentateuch (here and there from Exodus 20 through Deuteronomy 31) was adapted to changing circumstances and deepening understanding. For example, rules about animal sacrifice and appropriate places to worship developed over time. The changes were incorporated *into* the legal material associated with Moses rather than replacing it. It was as if the American people modified the Constitution not by adding amendments but by subtly inserting additions into the body of the Constitution, so that these later alterations looked as though they had been written by James Madison and Alexander Hamilton.

The books of prayer and reflection were expanded. Later contributors sometimes added new levels of meaning by adding new introductions. Two instances:

* Many psalms originated as songs to be prayed publicly in the temple. As the prayers were collected in the Book of Psalms, they developed a second use as meditative prayers to accompany individual study of Scripture. Psalm 1 was placed at the beginning of the collection to highlight this new purpose. "Blessed is the man who walks not in the counsel of the wicked ... but his delight is in the law of the Lord, and on his law he meditates day and night" (Psalm 1:1-2, RSV). Thus Psalm 1 presents to the person who opens the Book of Psalms the ideal of the individual who privately reads and ponders these prayers as God's written word.

- Ordinary people distilled their experience of the world into pithy sayings. Editors gathered these memorable maxims into what became the central chapters of the book of Proverbs (Proverbs 10–24). Later editors then composed an introduction to the proverb collection that speaks of God as the source of wisdom (Proverbs 1–9).

  Thus the book of Proverbs has a complex message. The proverbs themselves testify to the innate human capacity to learn from experience. They spur us to open our eyes and perceive how the world operates.

  At the same time, the opening chapters remind us that all wisdom, including everything we learn from experience, comes ultimately from God. Wisdom is his gift to those who revere him. Thus the book spurs us to seek God, to be humble toward him, to remember that his wisdom is greater than ours.

The prophets sometimes expressed views that were in tension with earlier tradition; for example, compare Exodus 34:6-7 with Ezekiel 18:14-20. Sometimes divergent views have been incorporated into the prophetic writings. For instance, anticipations that God would bring judgment on neighboring nations (Zecariah 14:12-15) were juxtaposed with predictions that he would call the nations to himself in a new covenant (Isaiah 19:19-25).

Implications of the Process

The Bible's long, complex processes of development—oral traditions, writing, rewriting, and editing—produced a book considerably different from any other. In the following chapters, we will consider some implications of its distinctiveness.

- While the historical books of the Bible recount actual events, the manner in which the events were transmitted has yielded narratives that are considerably different from modern history writing. (See chapter four, "Did It Really Happen?")

- As a result of its composition by many people in various places and times, the Bible displays contrasting emphases and insights. If Scripture were a piece of music, it would not be a violin solo but a symphony, with many interweaving musical motifs and even some discords. Since it bears the marks of successive generations' views and concerns, we might well ask, where is the Bible's source of unity? What makes it one book, not just a library of books?

  The Bible's source of unity does not lie in any of its human authors, none of whom grasped the whole. Rather, the Bible's unity comes from its one divine Author, who guided the community and, in a particular way, guided those who passed on the traditions and wrote and edited the biblical books. He was the composer who scored the whole grand symphony. (See chapter five, "Whose Words Are These?")

- As a crystallization of the traditions of a community, the Bible belongs to the community within which it developed. The Bible is the community's lasting testimony to its experience of God. It was designed to enable the community to continue to orient itself toward God, who continues to relate to this community.

  Thus, while anyone at all is welcome to pick up the Bible and read it, it can be adequately understood only within the community of faith. Only in this community does Scripture fulfill its fundamental purpose as God's instrument for making him known to his people. (See chapter six, "Whose Book Is This?")

- To be understood properly, the Bible needs to be read with an eye to the meaning expressed by its many human authors and editors, but also with an eye to what its one divine Author intended to communicate. The Bible's message as God's word to us comes into focus when we read it in light of God's perfect self-revelation of himself in Jesus Christ. (See chapter seven, "How Do We Know What It Means?")

Chapter Four

Did It Really Happen?
The Historical Authenticity of the Bible

The Bible is historical. It is concerned with what God has done in history and it communicates a great deal of historical information. But at no point is it quite like modern historical writing, and at some points it is quite different. The biblical writers belonged to cultures that wrote about the past differently from historians today. The historical material in the Bible bears the marks of the cultures in which it was written.

Ancient historians were different from modern ones both in regard to their resources and in regard to their approach.

Sources

While ancient historians could draw on historical sources that have since disappeared, they did not have access to the accumulations of literary and archeological data, the museums of artifacts, the vast numbers of books, journals, and other resources that modern historians have at their disposal. Typically, their sources consisted of oral traditions and a few documents. Thus, in many cases ancient writers could not discover details of time and place and quantity or the precise words that people had spoken. Often they were not able to quote verbatim, cite exact figures, or report precisely when and in what sequence events occurred.

As a result, the biblical histories leave unanswered many questions we might ask. What was the name of the Pharaoh who oppressed the

Hebrews? What was the date of the exodus from Egypt? Did Moses' views of God change over the years? What was the cultural, linguistic, and political background of the peoples that the Israelites confronted in Canaan? How long did Jesus' ministry last? Did *his* thinking change over time? At what point in his public life did he attack the merchants in the Jerusalem temple: at the beginning (as in the Gospel of John) or the end (as in the other Gospels)? What were his precise words of blessing over the bread and wine on the night before his death? The biblical authors do not give us answers (or they give us different answers) to these questions, either because the precise answers were not important to them or because they had no way of knowing for sure.

Approach

Modern historians examine the context of events—the political, economic, and social background of the people whose actions they relate. They are interested in processes by which individuals, institutions, and ideas changed. They try to view conflicts from the perspectives of both sides.

Ancient historians, by contrast, were less concerned with exploring the background of events or with tracing the development of personalities and groups or with presenting competing points of view. Their chief concern was to narrate events in ways that exhibited their present meaning for their readers. To accomplish this goal, they felt freer than modern writers to shape, omit, combine, and supply details.

For example, they might place their own words in speakers' mouths in order to express the speakers' views more fully. They would sometimes use poetic, even mythic language and imagery to highlight events. They might condense several distinct events into a single story.

Using a Little Imagination

Ancient writers incorporated poetry and poetic images in historical works in ways that modern historians would never think of doing. The imaginative way that ancient people were accustomed to dramatize historical events can be seen, for example, in David's prayer after he survives battles and achieves victory in wars against hostile peoples (2 Samuel 22; Psalm 18). David's thanksgiving speaks of God coming in storm and earthquake to rescue him from drowning in floodwaters. Obviously, this is David's poetic way of expressing how close he came to being killed and how powerful God's help seemed to him, not a description of the actual battles he engaged in.

In ancient literature, this imaginative expression of events is found not only in poetic works such as prayers but also in historical narratives. Speaking of the extensive reversals of nature in the Book of Exodus, such as the ten plagues that afflict the Egyptians, two modern historians write: "Of course, we are not constrained to interpret such reports literally. But other ancient peoples also used similar mythic language and imagery to celebrate otherwise real (and momentous) historical events. Therefore, the incorporation of supernatural imagery was not just a convention of ancient fiction writing, but also one of ancient history writing."[1] Thus the presence of such imaginative elements does not detract from the historical value of biblical narratives.

From a modern point of view, ancient historians' approach may seem an inferior way to write history. We would like something less imaginative, more precise, dealing with a wider range of issues. But if we accept the fact that the biblical historians were people of their own times and places, who worked within the limitations of their cultures, we can appreciate them for what they were: good historians but different from our own.

The writers were honest men who strove to communicate the truth. Their narratives do not contain lies or deceptions. The historical writings they produced compare well with other history-writing of their period. Whatever their cultural approach and the limitations of their resources, they were able to establish a reliable testimony to God's deeds in history.

There is no single answer to the question "How historically reliable is the Bible?" for there is a wide variety of types of writing shelved in the Bible's historical section. The subject of the Bible's relationship with history is a deep ocean. Here all we can do is hydroplane quickly over its surface, making some brief observations on the historical character of various blocks of biblical material.

Genesis 1–11

These first chapters of Genesis do not consist of historical accounts. Rather they combine mythical, legendary, and historical elements in stories of a kind that would have been familiar to people in the ancient Near East but are unlike any literature in modern Western culture.

The closest parallel in our experience to these Genesis stories may be parables. Parables are imaginary stories that communicate a truth and spur us to think. That is roughly the type of story we find in Genesis 3, for example, where the first man and woman eat forbidden fruit. The resemblance between the early Genesis accounts and parables is only partial, however, for parables are fictional, while some actual events do lie behind the Genesis accounts, although conveyed in legendary and imaginative forms. There *was* a creation, an original sin, a first murder.

The Catholic Church makes no claim that the early chapters of Genesis are historical in the modern sense of the word. As the Pontifical Biblical Commission wrote in 1948, these narratives "relate in simple and figurative language, adapted to the understanding of mankind at a lower stage of development, the fundamental truths presupposed by the economy of salvation, as well as the popular description of the beginnings of the human race."[2]

Failure to grasp the nature of the stories in Genesis 1–11 has had unhappy consequences. Many Christians have resisted evolutionary theories of the development of species, especially our own, because they thought such theories contradicted the Genesis accounts of creation (Genesis 1–2).

The Genesis stories, however, do not attempt to describe biological processes of development. This is apparent, for example, when the narrator of Genesis offers two different descriptions of the process by which God brought humans into existence. Genesis 1 states that God "created" us by a simple command (1:27), using a Hebrew word that never refers to making one thing from another. Genesis 2 says that God "formed" a man from dust and "made" a woman from the man's rib, using words elsewhere applied to shaping pots from clay and building houses from stones (2:7, 22). Evidently the narrator was intent on communicating *that* God created humans; *how* God did it was not part of his message.

Since the Genesis accounts do not intend to convey scientific or historical information in the modern sense, they cannot be contradicted by scientific or historical findings. No biological discovery can disprove the Genesis message that God created the human race, since Genesis does not provide a scientific description of how God brought humans into existence.

Recognizing the parable-like quality of the Genesis accounts saves us from getting hung up in futile controversies. We are freed to focus on the meaning of the accounts: God created everything; humans turned away from God; God brings judgment on sin, but remains kindly disposed toward humankind; and so on.

Genesis 12–50

Elements of the accounts of Abraham, Sarah, and the other ancestors of Israel are very ancient. One sign of the stories' antiquity is that they portray these ancestors as following a lifestyle of traveling herders. They live in tents, cluster in small family groups, get into disagreements over wells and pasturage. Yet the later generations that wrote the accounts had left this lifestyle behind and lived settled lives in towns and cities. Thus these stories of journeying ancestors seem to contain memories of a real past, rather than simply reflections of the writers' present.

Another sign of genuine historical material in the stories of the ancestors is the evidence for their way of life that archaeologists have brought to light. Archaeologists have confirmed, for example, that at one period in Mesopotamia (modern Iraq) it was the practice for a childless wife like Sarah to give her female servant to her husband as a concubine to produce offspring in her name (Genesis 16:1-4).

Nevertheless, later generations seem to have heavily reworked the accounts of the ancestors. Parts of these narratives may not have been written down until the end of the southern monarchy and the exile in

Babylon, more than seven centuries after the fact. It is doubtful that the stories passed through such a long period of oral retelling without significant changes. Some of the stories of the ancestors may be regarded as legendary.

The upshot of these considerations is that there is a basis for thinking that the outline of the stories in Genesis 12–50 reflects actual events: God made promises to the ancestors of Israel and showed them his saving presence. But many of the details may be later elaborations designed to bring out the relevance of these events for later generations.

It is not important to determine the exact historical content of these accounts in order to read them as God's word. Despite questions about the historical value of these stories, they give us authentic pictures of God's providence and kindness toward flawed human beings—stories that are rich in meaning for us as we relate to this same God today.

Exodus, Leviticus, Numbers, Deuteronomy, Joshua, Judges

In the books after Genesis, too, the accounts went through a considerable period of oral transmission before reaching papyrus. Scholars raise many questions. Did *all* the descendants of Abraham, Isaac, and Jacob emigrate to Egypt and later depart with Moses as described in Exodus? Or did those who came out of Egypt join up with others who had not gone there and invite them to join the covenant that God had made with them? Was there an Israelite *invasion* of Canaan? Or did wandering Israelite herders gradually settle down and take up farming, perhaps bringing into their tribal association neighbors who were already in the land?

Questions such as these arise not only from archaeological evidence, which does not always confirm the biblical accounts, but also from the various strands of material in the Bible. For example, the Book of Joshua describes the Israelites as quickly conquering Canaan (supporting the invasion scenario), while the Book of Judges shows the Canaanites still firmly in control of the cities after the time of Joshua (suggesting a more gradual process of settlement and expansion).

Again, whatever the answers to these sorts of questions, the basic facts are secure. God led some enslaved people out of Egypt, revealed himself to them, and made a covenant with them. He brought about their residence in the region east and west of the Jordan River. As ordinary readers of the Bible, we may let the historians discuss the details of the narratives while we focus our attention on the meaning of these events for us.

1 and 2 Samuel

Compared to the material in the preceding books of the Bible, the Books of Samuel were written rather soon after the events they relate. The accounts of the prophet Samuel and King Saul may have been put in writing within a generation of their deaths. This probably accounts for the wealth of detail about David in these books, which far exceeds that concerning any other king in Israel. The narrative of the succession to David's throne (2 Samuel 9–20; 1 Kings 1–2) is a world-class piece of historical writing.

Yet materials from varied oral sources have been combined in the Books of Samuel, as can be seen from the multiple accounts of how David became king (1 Samuel 16:1-13; 16:14–17:58; 1 Samuel 18:1–2 Samuel 2:5). This kind of multiplicity would be out of place in a modern historical work.

1 and 2 Kings

The authors of Kings worked with written sources such as palace archives. Consequently their narratives contain a great deal of authentic historical material.

Before this period Israel is very rarely mentioned in the records of other nations. But beginning with the period covered by the Books of Kings, points in the biblical narratives can be checked against written sources outside the Bible. For example, some accounts in Kings can be correlated with records from ancient Assyria, an empire that wrought havoc on the northern and southern Israelite kingdoms. The Assyrian accounts confirm details in the Books of Kings, although the Assyrian and Israelite accounts do not always line up perfectly. Clearly the Israelite scribes told the story from their own point of view—as did their Assyrian counterparts!

1 and 2 Chronicles

The Books of Chronicles cover much the same ground as 2 Samuel and 1 and 2 Kings. In fact, the authors of Chronicles used the Books of Samuel and Kings as their main sources of information. By setting the accounts side by side, it is possible to get an idea of how the authors of Chronicles reworked the material they found in Samuel and Kings. The authors of Chronicles respected their sources but felt free to add and subtract in order to help readers of their own day see the meaning that these historical events held for them.

Ezra, Nehemiah, Maccabees

Written on the basis of still recent recollections and numerous documents, these later histories contain a great deal of authentic historical information. Nonetheless, scholars find many puzzles in these books, including the basic chronology of events. Did Ezra precede Nehemiah, or the other way around?

The author of 2 Maccabees gave his own account of the period recorded in 1 Maccabees 1–7. If you set the two accounts side by side, you can see how much each writer shaped his narrative to emphasize certain points—sometimes contrasting ones. The author of 2 Maccabees, for example, was less admiring of the Maccabee family than was the author of 1 Maccabees.

Ruth, Tobit, Judith, and Esther

Four short books "shelved" with the historical works in the Old Testament—Ruth, Tobit, Judith, and Esther—reflect historical situations to varying degrees, and perhaps even some actual events, especially Ruth. But they are largely imaginative works written to strengthen faith in God and provide models of behavior. This, of course, does not detract from their importance. Outside the Bible, some of the most profound and influential writings in the world have been works of fiction.

The Gospels

In order to understand the historical character of the Gospels, it is helpful to distinguish three time periods:

1. *The time of Jesus with his disciples.* During this time, the disciples observed and listened to their Master and remembered what he said and did. They probably did not write anything during this phase.

From Oral Traditions to Written Gospels

The bishops of the Second Vatican Council had this to say about the composition of the Gospels:

> After the Lord's ascension, the apostles handed on to their hearers those things which he had said and done, with the fuller understanding they enjoyed once they had been instructed by the glorious events of the risen Christ's life and by the light of the Spirit of truth. The sacred authors wrote four gospels, choosing certain things from the many which had been handed on orally or had already been put in writing, condensing certain things into a synthesis or explaining them in view of the situation of the churches, and retaining the form of preaching but always in such a way that they communicated to us the honest truth about Jesus.
>
> *Dogmatic Constitution on Divine Revelation* (19)[3]

2. *The time of oral tradition and the first written reports.* After Jesus' ascension, the disciples pondered his life and death in light of his resurrection and spoke about him to others. As we have seen, during this period some Christians began to put elements of the traditions about Jesus into writing (see pages 37–38). But for the most part, the traditions about Jesus were conveyed in spoken words. The oral nature of the traditions about Jesus may have affected the accounts in a variety of ways.

First, as Jesus' followers handed on the recollections of him in preaching and pastoral care, there would have been a tendency to omit details that did not serve the purposes of ministry. The accounts of Jesus' life were often divested of names, places, dates, and other inessential details.

Second, as the preachers selected incidents for retelling on particular occasions, the individual incidents may have come to be remembered separately, apart from any overall chronology of Jesus' life. Likewise Jesus' teachings may have been communicated in short units of instruction. The situations in which he presented the teachings may have been forgotten. Thus the actual sequence of events in Jesus' life and the circumstances of his teachings may have become lost—although the traditions do seem to have passed on a connected narrative of Jesus' last days and hours.

Third, handed on by different groups of Christians in different places, the traditions about Jesus became somewhat varied. A single incident or instruction might be preserved in somewhat different forms (compare the miracle of loaves and fish in Luke 9:10-17 and John 6:1-14).

3. *The time of writing of the Gospels.* Finally, several writers composed the Gospels, working from both oral traditions and written sources

(which are no longer extant). Few scholars think that any of Jesus' original disciples were directly responsible for writing the Gospels (for Luke's Gospel, see Luke 1:1-4), although a few defend the view that the Gospels of Matthew and John come directly from Jesus' disciples.

Faithful Portraits of Jesus

Holy Mother Church has firmly and with absolute constancy held, and continues to hold, that the four Gospels ... whose historical character the Church unhesitatingly asserts, faithfully hand on what Jesus Christ, while living among men, really did and taught for their eternal salvation....

Dogmatic Constitution on Divine Revelation (19)[4]

Like those who had handed on the traditions about Jesus by word of mouth, the Gospel writers (often called "evangelists") wished to help people believe in Jesus and follow him. They were not scholars writing for other scholars but men with pastoral purposes—and the pastoral needs of their particular communities were somewhat different from each other. Furthermore, the evangelists had access to somewhat different traditions about Jesus.

As a result, each of the evangelists composed a somewhat distinctive portrait of Jesus. The sequence of events is somewhat different in each Gospel, possibly because each evangelist created a chronological framework for the smaller units of material that he had received from the tradition. Thus, with the exception of the accounts of Jesus' last supper, suffering, and death, the Gospels may not represent the actual order of events in Jesus' life.

Of course, there are close similarities as well as differences between the Gospels. Some of the similarities are due to parallels in the traditions upon which the writers drew. Some similarities are apparently due to the fact that one or two of the Gospel writers used the work of another. But who used whom is a matter of disagreement among scholars. Most scholars think that Matthew and Luke drew on Mark as a source, that Matthew and Luke had another written source in common ("Q"—see page 37), and that Matthew and Luke each had an additional, different, source of information. A few scholars, however, maintain that Luke drew on Matthew and Mark drew on Luke. There is debate over whether John was acquainted with the other three Gospels.

How historically reliable was the outcome? Obviously, like the rest of biblical history, the Gospels are not written as modern history. But there is every reason to think that those who handed on the oral traditions and committed these traditions to writing communicated a genuine picture of Jesus. I can mention only a few types of evidence here.

First, while the evangelists wanted to show the relevance of Jesus to readers of their own day, there are indications that they refrained from achieving this goal by manufacturing incidents and putting words into his mouth.

The evangelists, for example, did not manufacture material to deal with the greatest pastoral and theological crisis of their day: Should Gentiles be admitted directly into the Christian community or should they become Jews first, undertaking to follow the Mosaic law? This issue touched on the Church's basic understanding of Jesus and its own identity. Yet, since the question had not arisen during Jesus' lifetime, there was nothing in the traditions about him that directly answered it. Those who preached or wrote down the traditions about Jesus might have been tempted to make up some statements by him that would resolve the controversy. But the evangelists did not do this, although they seem to have gone out of their way to highlight traditions that shed light on the issue, for example, incidents in which Jesus welcomed Gentiles.

Second, the evangelists retained material that had lost its original relevance. During his ministry, Jesus frequently confronted challenges to his approach to keeping the Sabbath rest. By the time the evangelists wrote the Gospels, however, this was no longer a burning issue for most Christians, since most Christians of their day were not Jews and did not live in Palestine, where Sabbath-keeping was a normal part of the culture. Nevertheless, out of faithfulness to the tradition, the evangelists preserved many accounts of Jesus' controversies with fellow Jews about Sabbath observance.

Third, the evangelists preserved material that they might have found embarrassing. Most notably, they reported incidents that put Jesus' closest followers in an unfavorable light, for example, Peter's denial of Jesus (John 18:15-18, 25-27). Since those close followers became the leaders of the early Church, there would have been a strong motivation to purge the Gospels of accounts of their incomprehension, resistance, lack of faith, and infidelity to Jesus. But the Gospels were not "cleansed" in this way.

Thus the evangelists declined to create material about Jesus that might have been convenient and retained material that might have seemed useless or awkward. This is evidence of their respect for the traditions about Jesus that they had received. While the evangelists, like the gospel preachers before them, reshaped the traditions about Jesus in order to serve people in their own day, they were honest men who did not falsify their materials. They produced accounts of Jesus that both presented him faithfully and brought out his meaning for a later generation.

Given the way the material about Jesus had been handed on by word of mouth before being written down, the Gospels do not necessarily give us Jesus' precise words. Thus, for example, the wording of the Our Father is different in Matthew and Luke. The four Gospels relate the events of Jesus' ministry in somewhat different sequences. Given the way the differences between the Gospels are rooted in different oral traditions, it is not possible to determine exactly what Jesus' original words were or to produce a neat synthesis of the four Gospels that puts all the incidents in a single order—although many people have attempted to do this over the centuries.

But the differences in details and sequences between the Gospels do not make them unhistorical. The evangelists give us Jesus' words and deeds as they were conveyed in the preaching of the early Church by those who had known him. By recording the portrait of Jesus present in the apostolic preaching, the written Gospels bring us very close to Jesus' words and deeds—as close as the men and women were able to get who listened to the apostles' preaching. Corinthians who heard Paul's preaching in A.D. 51 and we who read the written Gospels today are equally recipients of the apostolic announcement of Jesus Christ.

As the biblical scholar Fr. Raymond E. Brown pointed out, the fourfold Gospel tradition creates a multidimensional picture of Jesus. The four Gospels enable us to see Jesus from different angles. Although the differences between the Gospels might have cast a shadow over their reliability, the early Church regarded the fourfold Gospel as a treasure rather than an embarrassment. When a second-century Syrian Christian named Tatian tried to synthesize the four Gospels into a single narrative, the Church insisted instead on preserving the four distinct written versions of the apostolic preaching about Jesus.

Acts of the Apostles

Archaeologists and historians have found much to confirm the historical nature of Luke's history of the early Church. The exact titles of government officials, the location of political boundaries, local customs, judicial procedures—Luke gets such details right. Careful investigation of Acts suggests that Luke had various sources to draw on, and that he followed his sources carefully.

Yet Luke recounted events as an ancient, not a modern, historian. Studies indicate that he followed the conventions of his time for writing history and biography. For example, the speeches of Christian leaders as they appear in Acts are probably a synthesis of historical material that Luke received and his own re-creation of what the speakers might have said. Overall, when compared to the historical works of his contemporaries, Luke's account of the early Church stands up well.

Chapter Five

Whose Words Are These?
The Bible's Divine and Human Dimensions

God acted in the lives of the people of Israel. He acted above all through Jesus of Nazareth. He continued to act in the early Church. At every step, God was revealing himself in both deeds and words.

God demonstrated his compassion and power, graciousness and justice, faithfulness and generosity through his involvement in people's lives—through events. At the same time, God communicated an understanding of his actions—and this understanding was necessarily conveyed in words.

The events through which God worked could effectively reveal him only if accompanied by divine interpretation. Without God's interpretation of events, it would have been impossible to grasp what he was doing—or even that he was doing anything at all. The sight of a ragged band of people fleeing across a marsh into the Sinai desert, the sight of a man hanging on a cross: How could an observer know that God was rescuing slaves in order to make a covenant with them or that he was receiving his Son's offering of his life as an atonement for the human race? God revealed himself through his actions at the Reed Sea and on Golgotha, but his interpretation was needed to complete the revelation.

Conversely, God's deeds confirmed his words. The return of Jewish exiles from Babylon and their rebuilding of the Jerusalem temple (Ezra 1–6) fulfilled God's promise that he would bring his people home and restore them (Jeremiah 30). The healings that the Spirit accomplished through the apostles demonstrated the authenticity of their preaching about Jesus (Acts 3–4).

The Bible came into being from the intertwined phenomena of God's words interpreting his deeds and his deeds confirming his words. The historical books of the Old Testament began to form around events in which the Israelites perceived God's hand at work. The prophetic books of the Old Testament preserved the messages of men who presented God's view of his people's condition and alerted them to how God was going to act in their regard. The events and the understandings were remembered, handed on orally, put into writing, rewritten, and edited. As we have seen, similar processes were at work, over a shorter period of time, in the writing of the New Testament, which bears witness to the life, death, and resurrection of Jesus and explains the significance of his coming for us.

God revealed himself in deeds and words to bring people into relationship with himself. The sacred writings that attest to his revelation have this same purpose. The Bible so well reflects God's revelation of himself to his people through words and deeds that it continues to be

---

Written So We Might Have Life

We declare to you what was from the beginning, what we have heard, what we have seen with our eyes, what we have looked at and touched with our hands, concerning the word of life—this life was revealed, and we have seen it and testify to it, and declare to you the eternal life that was with the Father and was revealed to us—we declare to you what we have seen and heard so that you also may have fellowship with us; and truly our fellowship is with the Father and with his Son Jesus Christ. We are writing these things so that our joy may be complete.

1 John 1:1-4

the instrument through which he speaks to us and acts in our lives.

Before my wife and I got married, I used to write her letters. She lived just the other side of town, but that seemed so far away! So I wrote her letters containing poems, lists, ponderings on my life, on what I thought of her, on what I hoped for our life together.

She has the letters stashed away in a closet. To her, they have some meaning, but I doubt they would be of much interest to anyone else (although I suspect the children might like to get a look at them). The letters were not written to supply material for anyone composing an anthology of literature or a social history. They are not literary or historical documents. They are simply love letters.

Basically, that is what the Bible is too. The Bible is God's means of communication with human beings. In the Bible, God has shown the kind of person he is and what he is about in the world, what he thinks about us and what he hopes for us, so that we might live in a relationship with him.

The purpose of the Bible is not that we should have a lot of information about God, let alone that we should have information about the history and culture of the ancient Near East. The purpose of the Bible is that, through knowing God's words and deeds, we would recognize his love for us. God gives us this book in order to give us himself.

The Bible achieves its purpose, then, only in the context of a love relationship between God and us. Historians can troll in the biblical books for data regarding ancient Near Eastern events; linguists are free to sift it for specimens of ancient languages. These uses are fine, as far as they go. But to treat the Bible only as a source of historical or linguistic information, or merely as an anthology of ancient literature, or even as a compendium of religious wisdom, misses the point. In the Bible, God wishes to meet us.

A Personal Word

We would be misled if revelation were taken to mean primarily certain facts or truths about God and religion. Revelation is primarily God's personal communication of himself to his children. You might know everything about God, but not know God; you would not have received his revelation. God's plan is part of revelation, but it is the second part. The first part is God himself.

Jerome Kodell, O.S.B.[1]

Truths Revealed

By his actions in history and his words to us, God has made clearer and more accessible some truths that we might possibly have managed to discover in other ways. God had already revealed himself simply by creating. Thus we could reason from effect to cause—from the existence, order, and beauty of the universe to the existence of One who is infinitely powerful and wise (Romans 1:18-20). From an examination of ourselves, we could reach a conclusion about the goodness of God, since our conscience, the moral compass built into us, is evidence of a just Creator.

But this kind of reasoning is difficult, and most of us are not inclined to think long and hard about such matters. Moreover, we are easily confused by the cacophony of voices in the world around us, promoting divergent views ("there are many gods," "nothing certain can be known about God," "there is no God"). Besides, we have an inclination to look at the world in terms of our self-interest, and our self-interest blinds us to the presence of a God who summons us away from selfishness. For these reasons, it is helpful that God has specially revealed even the basic truths about himself that he already manifested through creation.

In fact, God has revealed more to us than we could have known by our reasoning. Through his dealings with Israel and the Church he has shown us that we are designed for a personal relationship with him (having been created in his image—Genesis 1:26). He has revealed that his plan for us centers on his Son's becoming a human being, dying, and rising from the dead (a "mystery," or secret, now unveiled by God—Ephesians 1:9). Without his telling us, we could not have known that God has destined us, body and soul, for unending life with himself. Nor could we have known that, while being one God, he is Father, Son, and Holy Spirit. By reason alone, we might have come to grasp the principle that we should always treat others as we wish them to treat us. But without divine revelation we would probably not have grasped that self-sacrificing love is the dynamic by which we may attain the personal fulfillment for which we are created.

It is worth noting that the boundary between what we can know of God through our reason and what we can know only if God specially reveals it to us is not easy to draw. In a sense, all our knowledge of God comes through both the working of our minds and God's revealing himself to us. Our minds can discover any truth about God only because God is willing to allow us to know him. All our knowledge of God is a gift from him.

Inspiration

Who but God is able to identify and interpret God's activities in the midst of human affairs? Who but God is able to predict the course of action that God is going to take? Who but God is able to reveal the overarching plan that God is pursuing through human history? Obviously, only God. Thus, if the Bible is the written vehicle of God's revelation of himself and his plans for us, it must in some sense be God's word. But then, since Scripture was written by human authors, these human authors of Scripture have written God's word. How is that possible?

The answer is that God guided the authors and editors of the biblical books: He "inspired" them. As they observed, pondered, wrote, and edited, God communicated his thoughts to their minds and hearts. Inspiration involved a mysterious cooperation between God and human beings. God guided the thinking and writing of certain people of Israel and the early Church so that their words would faithfully bear witness to his deeds and communicate his understanding.

Just how the infinite God interacted with finite creatures to accomplish this is beyond our understanding. Somehow God uttered his words in the authors' depths, at the level of mind and heart where humans hunger for God. God guided them by revealing himself to them. By his Spirit, he directed them not by merely putting thoughts into their heads but by communicating his life, his truth, to them.

Receiving inspiration does not seem to have required any particular mental or emotional condition on the part of the human participants. Certainly the authors and editors of the biblical books were not of any one personality type. Their works display a variety of temperaments and moods—and also a variety of abilities. Among the biblical authors are theological geniuses, master storytellers, and world-class historians. But there are also some merely so-so poets, writers of labored prose, and an editor who was uncomfortably conscious of his limitations (2 Maccabees 15:38). God inspired them all.

Divine inspiration was not dictation. The human participants were not floppy discs on which God filed his data. They were authors in the full sense of the term. The thoroughly human quality of their writing is apparent in every line they produced, no matter how sublime or profound. Their works were fully their own. Yet, at the same time, their works were fully inspired by God. Thus the Bible is the words of God in the words of human beings.

The mystery of inspiration is all the more profound for being non-miraculous, in the sense that God did not override nature. He did not suspend the human participants' normal functions in order to speak through them. As theologian Dom Celestin Charlier observed, "Biblical writers wrote as other men do, and left the imprint of their personality on their work. For the most part they were not even conscious that they were inspired. Inspiration must not therefore be thought of as a substitution of God's action for the normal activity of the writer."[2]

In whatever way it operated, God's inspiration of the human authors was effective. God guided them and protected them from error—with the qualification that in the Old Testament God was moving his people progressively closer to the truth that would appear fully only in Christ. The result of inspiration is that, as the bishops at Vatican Council II stated, "the books of Scripture must be acknowledged as teaching solidly, faithfully, and without error that truth which God, for our salvation, wanted to be put into sacred writings."[3]

As New Testament scholar Abbot Jerome Kodell has written, inspiration assures us that when we open the Bible, we "are in the presence of God and his truth."[4] Despite the limitations of human words and concepts, God succeeded in conveying through Scripture the truth that he wanted us to have so that we might know and love him.

While Scripture is the result of a mysterious cooperation between God and human beings, the two parties are not authors in an equal way. God is the principal author of the Bible. For more than a thousand years, each of the human writers and editors took his turn composing his particular part of the biblical material and then left the scene. But God was the author from beginning to end.

In order to communicate with us, God shaped his words to our capacity to hear and understand. He used human words and concepts. He accommodated himself to our limited comprehension, like a parent bending down to speak to a small child.

Written by God

Holy Mother Church ... holds that the books of both the Old and New Testament, in their entirety, with all their parts, are sacred and canonical because, having been written under the inspiration of the Holy Spirit ... they have God as their author.
Dogmatic Constitution on Divine Revelation (11)[5]

While God limited himself to working within the narrow range of our understanding, however, he allowed himself full freedom as to the types of human communication he employed. God did not confine himself to inspiring only historical narratives. God could and did inspire authors to work in a wide variety of forms—legal codes and hymns, love songs and genealogies, letters, short stories, prophetic oracles, and others.

Divine inspiration guarantees that a piece of writing is true. The inspired text communicates God's message. Inspiration does not mean that the writing is necessarily factual. Other forms of writing, for example, poems and fictional stories, can be true in their own way, as we can easily see from such familiar examples as Psalm 23 ("The Lord is my shepherd ...") and the parables of Jesus ("There was a man who had two sons ...").

God was at liberty to inspire whatever kind of writing he chose. In parts of the Bible, he chose to use the types of historical writing that were composed in the ancient Near East. These kinds of historical writing, as we have seen, are somewhat different from modern historical writing. In inspiring the biblical historians, God did not turn them into modern-style history writers. Rather, he used their ancient types of history writing to convey what he intended.

We have seen how complex were the Bible's origins. God's inspiration was correspondingly complex. He guided those who passed on the traditions by word of mouth. He guided those who wrote and those who reshaped and rearranged what was written. He guided those who edited and assembled the completed works. In sum, God inspired the entire process by which the Bible came to be.

A Living Word

Scripture not only *was* inspired; it remains inspired—"God-breathed," as the author of 2 Timothy 3:16 literally says. As we read Scripture, the God who created us to know and love him brings his words to life for us. Just as the Spirit revealed God to the authors in their deepest being, their words speak to us in our deepest being. As we read the Bible, God corrects our vision, straightens out our thinking, shakes us free from illusions and self-delusions, opens our eyes to the light of Christ, gives us a longing for his kingdom.

The Spirit that inspired the writers of the Old Testament became fully present in Jesus. That same Spirit now fills us as we read the Scripture that bears witness to him. The Spirit reveals the Son, who is the perfect revelation of the Father. As we read, the Spirit draws us into the love-relationship within God, in which the Father loves and gives everything to the Son, and the Son loves and returns everything to the Father.

Because Scripture is God's word to all people, each of us may expect God to speak to us through it. God's word is powerful, as we see in the Bible when prophets speak and, above all, when Jesus speaks (consider,

---

A Powerful Word

God's word, in whatever form it comes, always has divine healing and saving power. The seven sacraments of the Church are the most vivid and direct proclamations of God's healing word in Christ. The risen Lord Jesus acts in them to extend his healing touch to the minds, hearts, and bodies of the disciples. Where conditions are right, that is, where a heart is open in faith, the seed of God's word takes root and has a sure effect. The same kind of divine power is available through God's written word in the Bible; the effect of individual readings is not as clearly defined, but the healing power of God is present. It is "the word of God at work within you who believe" (1 Thessalonians 2:13).

Jerome Kodell, O.S.B.[6]

---

for example, his words of command—Mark 1:41-42; 4:39; 5:41-42; 7:34-35). As God's word, the Bible is a channel of God's power. As

God leads us to know him and understand his ways through Scripture, his Spirit changes us.

Because the Bible brings us into contact with the living God, reading it will take us beyond our expectations. Scripture will confront us where we are least prepared, call us to change where we are most reluctant to try, give us comfort and hope where none can be seen. God gives us his word so we might understand his ways and be joyful in responding to him, even in suffering. Through Scripture he calls us to live in ways that we would not have envisioned apart from his word. He enables us to make our way through earthly life to a greater life yet to be revealed.

Chapter Six

Whose Book Is This?
The Bible in the Church

God's life-giving revelation of himself reached its climax in the becoming-flesh of the divine Word. Jesus himself is the perfect revelation of God. To look at Jesus is to see the Father (John 14:9). Jesus is God's complete word to the human race (Colossians 1:15-20; Hebrews 1:1-4). In Jesus, God has expressed himself to us as fully and clearly as he can. He has said all he can say. God has no further word to speak to us.

Surely God wants the definitive revelation that he has given us to continue on in the world in a way that accomplishes his life-giving purpose. It is unthinkable that God would let his Word enter the world only to have the report and understanding of his coming fade away and become lost amid a babble of human voices. God intends his ultimate revelation of himself in Jesus to continue to be accessible to all men and women throughout the rest of history.

God ensures the continuing testimony to Jesus in the world through the Holy Spirit (John 14:15-26; Acts 1:4-8). But the Spirit must have means to accomplish his purpose. What means does the Spirit use?

Obviously one instrument of the Spirit is the Bible. As a piece of writing, the Bible offers a stable, unchanging witness to the incarnate Word. It gives us the inspired key to understanding the meaning of Jesus' life, death, and resurrection.

Yet precisely because it is a written document, the Bible alone is not sufficient to provide an authentic, life-giving testimony to God's revelation of himself in Jesus. No book, not even a divinely inspired one, can interpret itself. Books are interpreted by people. As long experience demonstrates, different people may interpret the Bible in vastly different ways. This phenomenon arose already in the New Testament period (2 Peter 3:15-16). The conflict of meanings that various interpreters have derived from the Bible raises the question as to whether its authentic meaning can be known with certainty. This is a question of enormous importance. If it were to become impossible to determine which interpretations of the Bible were authentic, the revelation which the Bible is designed to communicate would become less accessible to us. Along with the divinely inspired Bible, then, something else is needed: a divinely inspired interpreter.

Furthermore, no book by itself can achieve God's goal of drawing us into his life through his Son. True, *this* book contains the inspired testimony to God's offer of life through Jesus. But if we are seeking God, we need more than words that bear witness to Jesus; we need living witnesses—persons who can testify to personal knowledge of the risen Jesus.

All this means that the Bible needs a *community* that is divinely guided in interpreting it and divinely empowered to live the life about which it speaks. This community exists. It is the Church. The Church is the central instrument of the Spirit, by which God makes his revelation of himself in Jesus Christ present in the world.

By the power of the Spirit, the Church's preaching and worship and its members' lives of love, goodness, service, and self-sacrifice bear witness to the reality of Jesus' life, death, and resurrection. In the words and actions of Christians, we have the opportunity to encounter Jesus in a living way. Through the Church's sacramental ministry, we can experience the reconciliation with God that he has opened up through Jesus' death and resurrection. Thus the bishops at Vatican Council II called the Church the "sign and instrument" of the saving, self-revealing work that God has accomplished through Jesus, by which human beings may be united with God and one another.[1]

Guided by the Spirit, the Church is the authentic interpreter of Scripture and the living witness to the risen Lord. This is an enduring reality. Jesus guaranteed his presence with the Church until the end of time (Matthew 28:20). God has given the Church his Spirit, to guide it and keep it in the truth (John 14:15-26). Of course, all of us who are members of the Church sin and err; but God protects the Church as a whole from losing the truth and holiness that he has given it in Christ.

> What was handed on by the apostles includes everything which contributes to the holiness of life and the increase in faith of the people of God; and so the Church, in her teaching, life, and worship, perpetuates and hands on to all generations all that she herself is, all that she believes.
>
> *Dogmatic Constitution on Divine Revelation* (8)[2]

Jesus provided a key element for maintaining the Church in faithfulness to himself when he authorized a group of men to be his representatives. These were his "apostles," that is, "those sent" by him (Mark 3:13-19). During his ministry, Jesus gave them access to himself and trained them as his disciples so that they would be able to live as he lived and communicate his message accurately and effectively. He prepared them to be the leadership group for his community, the foundation for its ongoing life (Matthew 10:1–11:1) and designated Peter as the leader of this group of leaders (Matthew 16:13-19; Luke 22:31-32; John 21:15-19).

The apostles carried out this commission, by the power of the Spirit. In turn, they handed on this commission to men who came after them. As a result, the preaching of the gospel that began when Peter addressed the crowd in Jerusalem at the beginning of the Church's existence (Acts 2) has never fallen silent. The apostolic preaching has resounded in the Church down through the centuries. God's word has continued in the Church as a living tradition, through the handing on of the teaching of Christ and the life in the Spirit from one generation to the next. Through the Church, God will make his ultimate revelation of himself in Jesus accessible to all men and women throughout the rest of history.

While the leaders of the community play a special role in maintaining the Church in faithfulness to the Lord, every member plays a part. Not only the leaders but the entire Christian community share in handing on God's revelation in Christ. The living tradition about Jesus is passed on by Christians as they study, contemplate, celebrate, and live the gospel.

In the early Church period we see the whole Christian community handing on the word of God by letting his word reshape their lives, by acting on it, by publicly acknowledging it, by presenting it to others in their ordinary circumstances (see 1 Thessalonians 1:2-10). The Greek or Roman person who, on hearing the gospel, stopped worshiping

What's a Canon?

The term *canon* comes from a Semitic word for "reed." Since reeds were sometimes used as measuring rods, the word came to have that meaning also. Applied to the Scripture, canon means that this collection of books is recognized as inspired by God in such a way as to serve as the norm—the regulating rule—for faith and moral teaching.

false gods and embraced the one God, the wealthy Christian family who opened their home to care for poor members of the community, the Christian couple who adopted an abandoned infant, the man or woman who accepted death rather than deny Christ—each of these embodied the life of Christ, each of them made visible the Word-made-flesh. They made the gospel accessible to others and passed on the faith to the next generation. The early Christian communities as a whole were a revelation of God to the world, a revelation written not on paper or stone, but on human hearts (2 Corinthians 3:2-3).

Canon

We can see the Church's role of authoritatively interpreting Scripture above all in the formation of the New Testament. The testimony to God's revelation in Jesus was at first communicated in the oral tradition of apostolic preaching and in the lives of all the members. Soon the tradition took written form. The early Christians recognized that writings that expressed the apostolic teaching would provide a reference point for later Christian thinking and acting. By the end of the first century, all, or virtually all, of the writings we now call the New Testament had been composed.

At the same time, there were other Christian writings in circulation—gospels, letters, revelations. The question inevitably arose: Which writings express the genuine tradition about Jesus? In the middle of the second century, a misguided Christian teacher named Marcion provoked the Church to provide an answer to this question. Marcion argued that the Church should regard only a very small number of writings as authoritative (Luke the only Gospel, no letters but a few of Paul's). By contrast, other Christian teachers were treating a much wider number of writings as authoritative.

> In discerning the canon of Scripture, the Church was also discerning and defining its own identity. Henceforth Scripture was to function as a mirror in which the Church could continually rediscover her identity and assess, century after century, the way in which she constantly responds to the gospel and equips herself to be an apt vehicle of its transmission.
>
> Pontifical Biblical Commission[3]

Gradually the Church sifted through its writings to identify which should constitute its authoritative collection concerning Jesus.[4] Church leaders selected writings that were considered to have been written by the apostles or by those who worked with them (Mark, for example, was believed to have drawn the material for his Gospel from the apostle Peter). Other crucial considerations were whether the writings were a genuine reflection of apostolic preaching, were in conformity with the "rule of faith" (the basic Christian convictions that became expressed in the creeds), and were used in the liturgy.

In the selection process, the leaders of the Church sought to identify the writings that expressed the faith that the Church already held and lived, the faith received from the apostles. The Church did not *discover* its faith in its writings. The Church had to *know* its faith in Christ in order to be able to recognize which writings faithfully reflected its faith.

The same Spirit that had guided writers to put the apostolic preaching about Jesus into written form guided these later leaders of the Church to recognize the writings that reliably conveyed that apostolic faith. Much later, Vatican Council I (1869–70) clarified the point that the New Testament writings are the authentic expressions of the faith not because the Church says so, but because the Church discerned that these writings have God as their author. The Church did not make the books of the Bible inspired; it acknowledged their inspiration.

By the end of the fourth century, Christians East and West had reached general agreement on the twenty-seven books that today constitute the New Testament for Catholics, Protestants, and Orthodox (Syrian, Egyptian, and Ethiopian branches of Christianity have slightly different New Testament collections). It was only at the Council of Trent (1545–63) that an ecumenical council formally defined these twenty-seven books as constituting the New Testament canon. But Trent was affirming what had been established for more than a thousand years.

Why Are Catholic and Protestant Bibles Different?

Even before the Church produced and canonized the writings that constitute the New Testament, it received the writings that constitute the Old Testament.

By the time of Jesus, certain writings had become recognized among Jews as Scripture. Jesus used and interpreted these writings as Scripture, and so did the early Church.

Questions inevitably arose in the Church, however, about precisely which writings belonged to this authoritative collection, because its limits had not been finally set by Jews in the time of Jesus. In the first century, Jews in Palestine used one set of books as Scripture; Greek-speaking Jews outside Palestine used these same books, but within a larger collection. This larger collection was in Greek and is often called the *Septuagint*, from the Greek word for "seventy," for it was said that the translation from Hebrew had been produced by seventy scholars.

Furthermore, neither the smaller Hebrew collection in Palestine nor the larger Greek collection seems to have been strictly defined at this time.

Since Christianity spread mainly within the Roman Empire, where Greek was the international language, Christians in the first three centuries generally used the larger, Greek collection. Meanwhile, by the second century, Jewish leaders in Palestine and elsewhere settled on the shorter set of books as used in Palestine. Why they did so is not entirely clear. It may have had something to do with language. The books in the shorter set were all in Hebrew and Aramaic, while some of the books in the longer set existed only in Greek. But language does not entirely account for the Jewish decision to embrace the shorter set, since some of the additional works in the Greek collection were originally composed in Hebrew or Aramaic (Sirach, 1 Maccabees, Tobit).

In the fourth century, some Christian teachers, including St. Athanasius and St. Jerome, thought the Church should limit its Old Testament to the shorter list of books that had established itself as the official Bible for Jews everywhere. Others, such as St. Augustine, maintained that the larger set of books in the Greek collection should be maintained as the Church's Old Testament on the basis of its longstanding Christian use. The book of Sirach, for example, was very widely quoted in the early Church.

St. Augustine's view proved persuasive. By the fifth century the Church in both East and West generally recognized the longer collection as its Old Testament (although East Syrian,

Egyptian, and Ethiopian Christians acknowledge a slightly different set of Old Testament books).

In the sixteenth century, the Protestant reformers advocated a return to the shorter Palestinian collection. They did this partly from a desire to exclude one of the books in the longer collection that was used by Catholics to defend the doctrine of purgatory, a doctrine which Protestants rejected (2 Maccabees 12:42-46). The Reformers may also have embraced the shorter canon because they thought it was the Scripture that Jesus used. In the sixteenth century, scholars were not aware that the canon of Scripture for Jews in first-century Palestine was still somewhat fluid.

In response to the Protestant reformers, in 1546 the Catholic bishops at the Council of Trent gave official recognition to the longer collection of books. Since the longer collection, the Septuagint, itself varied slightly from version to version, the bishops at Trent further specified exactly which writings constituted the Old Testament. They recognized all the books and parts of books that are found in the ancient Latin translation of St. Jerome (called the "Vulgate," or "ordinary language," version).

Tradition

We have seen that God guided the oral traditions that flowed into the Old and New Testaments and guided the authors and editors as they composed and refined the texts through various stages of development. He guided the early Christians as they sorted through the writings and determined which expressed their faith in Christ. But

God's guiding presence did not then come to a halt when the completed volumes of the New Testament were arranged on the shelves of the biblical library.

Jesus is Emmanuel—"God with us" (Matthew 1:23). Through the incarnation of his Word and the gift of his Spirit, God has established his presence among us. The Spirit's guidance now produces no new Scripture. Yet the Spirit, who is no less present now than he was in New Testament times, leads us into deeper understanding and new applications of Scripture.

God's Spirit has always been at work in the Church. As Jesus' followers have communicated their faith outward to other people and downward to successive generations, the Spirit has been involved at every step. The Spirit is the living principle, the power, in this "handing on."

The concept that comes into play here is that of *tradition,* which comes from the Latin word for "handing on." It is helpful to distinguish two aspects of this concept.

There is, first, tradition in the sense of the content: that which is handed on. The Bible is the written form of "that which is handed on" from Christ to the apostles and from the apostles to every later generation. Scripture is not all that is handed on. The revelation of Christ, known and lived in the Church, has been handed on in other forms also. Most notably, the Church has handed on its knowledge of Christ in its creeds (summary expressions of its faith), in its liturgy (its central acts of worship), and in the authoritative teaching of popes and councils.

There is, second, tradition in the sense of the process: the handing on. Tradition in this sense occurs in various ways: as the bishops preach and teach, as the Eucharist and the other sacraments are celebrated, as Christians profess their belief in Christ and live out their testimony to him by loving and serving their neighbors.

Obviously the content and the process go together within the community that knows and lives what it hands on. This has an important implication for understanding the Bible. Since the Scriptures are the written part of "that which is handed on" in this community of faith, it is only within this community of faith that the Bible's full meaning is accessible. Of course, the Bible is open to anyone who wishes to read it. But it belongs essentially to the Church that knows and lives by it.

A parallel to this relationship of text and community is the way that the Declaration of Independence and the Constitution belong to the people of the United States. If a person wishes to understand the Bill of Rights of the Constitution, for example, he or she needs to study how the courts of the United States have authoritatively interpreted those clauses over the last couple of centuries. In fact, the inquirer needs to live in the United States and experience those principles in operation in American society.

The Bible is the book of the Church. The Church is the Bible's home, because the Church is the community that has inherited the living tradition that perceives the Bible's meaning.

The authors of Scripture did not receive their inspiration as independent operators but as members of God's people. Correspondingly, God now inspires men and women to understand the Bible as they participate in the life of his people.

The central purpose of the Bible is to lead us to know God. We attain this purpose by entering into the knowledge of God that is present in the Church, among the followers of Jesus. We get in touch with Jesus Christ through the Church, which is his body (1 Corinthians 12:27; Ephesians 1:22-23). If we do not have some experience of God's forgiveness, mercy, humility, power, and glory from the life and worship of the Church, it will be difficult for us to understand what the Bible says about these realities.

To some people, the Church seems a confining context for interpreting Scripture. They would prefer a more neutral location from which to read. But there is no such neutral location. We all bring pre-suppositions with us when we come to read the Bible. Indeed, we interpret every piece of writing within some frame of reference. None of us is a blank slate—nor should we try to be. Learning something does not involve emptying our heads of everything we already know.

When we read the Bible, what will our interpretive framework be? We are all creatures of our culture, in ways that we ourselves never entirely understand. As Jerome Kodell puts it, if we do not take the Church as our authoritative guide to Scripture, we expose ourselves "to the danger of following, without realizing it, an unidentified authority." This might be "prejudice, materialism, or American common sense."[5]

To be correctly understood, Scripture must be explored in the context of the faith in which it was written, according to the intention of the Spirit who inspired its human authors. And the only way we can know that we are interpreting Scripture in the Spirit in which it was written is to read each part of it within the whole canon that the Church has assembled and to read the whole canon within the tradition of the Church's worship, teaching, and life.

There are two stages in the relationship between the Bible and Tradition. For the birth and growth of revelation, it was the Spirit's role to act on the living Tradition in such a way that it was gradually crystallized into Scripture. When revelation was complete in its written form, it was the Spirit's role to interpret it and continue to give it life by Tradition.

Celestin Charlier[6]

The Bible Applied to Life Today

In one sense, Scripture is complete. It is the Church's canon, the complete yardstick for measuring its teaching and practice. No further writings can be added to it. But the Bible is not the complete book of theology, the complete book of liturgy, the complete hymnbook, the complete guide to evangelism or marriage or fundraising. Not everything that we need to know for Christian faith and life is contained in Scripture in the form in which we need it.

The Bible is the norm for all later teaching, liturgy, sacraments. It is the "soul" of theology.[7] But the Bible does not contain the entire tradition of the Church.

The Bible does not answer all the questions we encounter about Christian living. What are the appropriate forms for private prayer and community worship? How do we apply Jesus' teaching about material possessions, about living as a servant of others, about trusting God? How can we be guided by the Spirit? How should Christians relate to the state?

To live a life that attains God's purposes, we need more than the Bible; we need wisdom, examples, guidelines, applications. This is where the traditions of the Church come in. The traditions of prayer and liturgy and sacramental celebration, the examples and writings of saints, the bishops' instructions about how to act as Jesus' followers in the world—all these form a living bridge between the Bible and the twenty-first century.

These traditions are hardly monolithic. The gospel has been appropriated in various ways in different cultures and ages. To be guided by these traditions in shaping our Christian lives does not mean walking a narrow path but swimming in a broad river.

In practice, the local church communities of diocese and parish, pastored by our bishop and priest, are the natural places for us to grow in understanding Scripture and applying it to our lives. In the parish, especially, we have the opportunity to read Scripture with others, to discuss, to listen to one another. Our pastors—some, of course, more than others—are gifted to guide us in our reflection on Scripture, so that we might discern what the Spirit is saying in our hearts and learn to respond.

In the parish setting we can listen to those whose grasp of Scripture may be simple but deeply lived. Sometimes the poorest, neediest members of the Church community, because they rely most directly on God's help, are able to hear and apply his word in a particularly acute way (James 2:5).

Teaching Authority

At points in our reading of the Bible, we need more than supplementary guidance to help us respond to God's word; we need authoritative clarification. Were Jesus' "brothers" also children of his mother Mary (Mark 6:3)? To what degree is Jesus present in the Eucharist (Matthew 26:26-28)? When Paul writes that "we are justified by faith" (Romans 5:1), does he mean that our own efforts to respond to God's grace play no role in our relationship with God? Does Jesus allow any grounds for divorce and remarriage in Matthew 5:31-32?

In the history of the Church such questions have given rise to considerable debate, because there seems to be more than one possible way to interpret what Scripture says. Thus it is a great blessing that Jesus commissioned his apostles to teach in his name (Matthew 16:17-19; Mark 3:13-19). With the guidance of the Spirit, the apostles and their designated successors—the popes and bishops—

have been able to provide answers to such questions.

In doing so, the popes and bishops have not added to the revelation given once and for all in Christ. Rather they have given authentic—that is, authorized—interpretations of that revelation. The bishops do not stand over Scripture as judges. Referring to the "teaching office"—the authorized interpretative role—of the pope and bishops, the bishops at Vatican Council II declared: "This teaching office is not superior to the Word of God."[8]

The Bible is the canon, the standard for the Church. But the Church needs an authorized body of leaders to apply the standard in an authentic way. This need is met by the teaching office of the bishops, who are the successors of the apostles. This teaching authority is termed the *magisterium*—from the Latin word *magister,* "teacher."

As George Martin points out in *Reading Scripture As the Word of God,* it makes no sense to accept the canon of Scripture defined by an authoritative Church leadership in the past, yet reject the same authoritative Church leadership in the present when it interprets the contents of that canon: "To do so would be to claim that the Holy Spirit who guided the early Church no longer guides the Church in our time."[9]

It is important not to exaggerate the extent to which the popes and bishops have given authoritative interpretations of particular passages of Scripture. In his 1943 statement on the study of the Bible (*Divino Afflante Spiritu*), Pope Pius XII observed that such authoritative interpretations are rather few. The magisterium does not tell us what everything in the Bible means.

Even when the magisterium speaks authoritatively about something in the Bible, it usually does not attempt to provide an exhaustive interpretation. It may simply declare that a certain interpretation of a passage is mistaken, as in its judgment that the thousand-year reign of Christ in Revelation 20 is not to be interpreted as an earthly event of one thousand actual years. The Catholic reader is free to explore other possible interpretations of this chapter. Sometimes the Church grounds a portion of its teaching in a specific passage of the Bible—as when it connects the sacrament of reconciliation with 1 John 1:5–2:2 and the sacrament of anointing with James 5:14-15. But such declarations do not attempt to expound the entire meaning of the passages in question. They leave room for further investigation.

Even when the leaders of the Church give an authoritative interpretation, they do so according to the same interpretative principles that should guide all members of the Church in understanding the Bible. To these principles of interpretation of Scripture we will turn our attention in the chapter that follows.

Is the Bible Self-Interpreting?

Many Protestants take the view that the Bible provides everything needed to interpret itself and that there is therefore no need for a magisterium to supply authoritative interpretation. Indeed, many Protestants see this as a crucial principle for safeguarding the authority of God's word, since it might otherwise fall under the authority of human interpreters.

But numerous interpretive issues arise in reading the Bible. Which statements are to be taken as straightforward statements of fact, and which are to be taken as metaphors and symbols? How do the various parts of the Bible relate to each other? How does the Old Testament speak about Christ, the Church, and Christian life? How are Old Testament prophecies to be applied to society today?

Whenever interpreters give answers to such questions, it becomes clear that they depend on some interpretive tradition. No reader develops an absolutely independent interpretation of the Bible. In practice, if readers are not guided by an authoritative Church tradition, they are guided, consciously or unconsciously, by some other interpretive framework.

A test case for whether the Bible is self-interpreting is the work of popular Protestant Bible teachers and prophecy experts regarding the end times and Jesus' second coming. These teachers insist that they are simply reading what the Bible itself says, without imposing human opinions on it. But the interpretations of these experts are by no means obvious. They claim to draw their elaborate scenarios for the end of world history from the Bible. But the scenarios are not found in the Bible. Rather, they are constructed by linking together widely separated statements in Daniel, Revelation, and other biblical books into a framework already present in the mind of the interpreter. In the process, individual biblical statements are given interpretations that are far from obvious.

The interpretive framework of the Bible prophecy experts stems from a tradition going back only to the nineteenth century. The interpreters' particular scenarios vary according to their individual preferences and personalities. But in every case the result is that the Bible is submitted to a set of assumptions that come from outside itself.

This is simply one illustration of the fact that no interpretation of the Bible comes simply from within the Bible. In biblical interpretation, as in all reading, the interpreter comes to the text with a certain viewpoint, with certain presuppositions.

The question is this: Which viewpoint and presuppositions will it be?

Far from interfering with the Bible's interpretation of itself, the Church's magisterium, which is in living continuity with the tradition that has come from the earliest period of the Church, is the best resource for approaching the Bible in a way that can arrive at its true meaning.

Chapter Seven

How Do We Know What It Means?
Interpreting the Bible

In the Bible, God has entered into what is human. The Bible is similar to that most profound divine entry into our human world—the
mystery of God taking on human nature in Jesus Christ. The bishops
at Vatican Council II wrote: "In sacred Scripture ... the words of God,
expressed in human languages, have become like human speech, just
as long ago the Word of the eternal Father, taking on the flesh of
human weakness, became like human beings."[1]

In Jesus, there is no division between the human and the divine.
His every action is both a human act and an act of God. Similarly, in
Scripture there is no division between God's words and the words of
human beings. God inspired the human authors, with the result that
what they said is what God said. Scripture is the message of God in
completely human form.

As we noted in a previous chapter, in the composition of the Bible,
God did not use the human authors as mere recording devices, passive
transmitters of words they did not understand. The men—and, if
there were any, the women—who produced the biblical writings used
their eyes and ears, their hearts and heads. As the bishops at the Second
Vatican Council thought: "To compose the sacred books, God chose
certain men who, all the while he employed them in this task, made
full use of their powers and faculties so that, though he acted in them
and by them, it was as true authors that they consigned to writing
whatever he wanted written."[2]

Since in the Bible God has spoken to us through men who were deliberate, thinking human communicators, we must grasp the meaning they deliberately and thoughtfully expressed if we are to understand the message that God wishes to convey to us. We cannot bypass the meaning of the human authors and meet God directly in some mystical way in the words of Scripture. While God has communicated more through Scripture than the individual human authors understood, the starting point for discovering his meaning is to discover the meaning they did understand and express. In the words of the bishops at Vatican II: "Since in sacred Scripture God has spoken through human beings in a human way, the interpreter of sacred Scripture, in order to ascertain what God wished to communicate to us, should attentively search out what the sacred writers actually intended to signify and God wished to reveal by their words."[3] This principle is the starting point for all interpretation of Scripture.

In seeking the meaning that the human authors communicated, we are trying to grasp their intention. St. Augustine wrote, "To understand the divine oracles properly, there must be a constant effort to reach the mind of the author. It is through him that the Holy Spirit has spoken."

But seeking the human authors' intention does not mean delving into the hidden recesses of their minds and speculating about what they wished but failed to say. We are looking for the meaning they actually embodied in their words.

In contemporary Catholic usage, the meaning that the authors expressed is called the *literal* meaning. It is important to see that the literal meaning is not what we might call the "face value" of the words. The literal meaning is the meaning that the words were designed to communicate, not a meaning that they might bear if read apart from or against their context.

So, for example, the literal meaning of a metaphorical text is the meaning of the metaphor. Thus, the literal meaning of "the Lord is my shepherd" (Psalm 23:1) is "God provides for me in every way"—not "I am a four-footed animal whom God pastures." When Jesus says if your hand leads you into sin, cut it off (Matthew 5:30), his literal meaning is not "amputate your hand" but "take radical measures." Interpretations that took the metaphors at face value—"God raises sheep," "chop off your hand"—might be called *literalistic*, rather than literal.

Actually, we should speak in the plural about Scripture's literal *meanings*. We all know how complex human communication can be. Even a straightforward business memo often has more than a single level of meaning.

Say, for example, that I receive an e-mail from my boss telling me to fly to Houston to close a deal. This simple instruction may carry overtones and undertones. Her choice of words may imply how important she thinks the deal is. The fact that she is sending the e-mail to me rather than to someone else in the office may suggest her confidence in my negotiating ability. If she knows that I would rather not travel, her directive may be a reminder that she's the boss.

If such a simple communication may have layers of meaning, the same is even more true of the Bible. In fact, the biblical writers packed their texts full of meanings. Density of meaning is typical of poetry, of which there is a great deal in the Bible. But the Bible's prose sections are heavy with meaning too.

One reason for this is that the authors were skillful, and often artistic, men who wrote complex works. Furthermore, that they were writing about profound, sometimes paradoxical, and ultimately mysterious realities, and the profundity, paradox, and mystery of their subject matter is reflected in their writings. Thus multiple levels of literal meaning confront us at every turn in the Bible. For example:

- Chapters 37 to 50 of Genesis tell us what happened to a young man named Joseph in Egypt. Yet the writer is doing more than merely entertaining us with a story about a young man in a fashionable coat. He has shaped his account of Joseph to steer us toward an insight into God's hidden guidance of our own lives. The message about God's unseen yet reliable presence with all of us is very much a part of the literal meaning of his well-told tale.

- Biblical laws are intended to regulate people's behavior. But, in addition, they instruct us in a system of values. A key Hebrew word for "law," *torah,* means "instruction." So, for example, "Thou shalt not kill" not only forbids killing. It teaches respect for human life (Exodus 20:13).

- The Book of Proverbs contains hundreds of pithy sayings. These proverbs convey people's life experiences in condensed form for our instruction. But the proverbs go beyond offering observations and warnings. Consider, for example, the placement of these two proverbs side by side (Proverbs 26:4-5): "Do not answer fools according to their folly, or you will be a fool yourself." "Answer fools according to their folly, or they will be wise in their own eyes." The literal meaning of this juxtaposition is that we must evaluate individual situations according to their unique characteristics.

- The Gospels relate numerous incidents in the life of Jesus. But they do much more than inform us. Episode after episode, the Gospels are composed in a way that invites to us to step into the story and relate to Jesus alongside the people in the narrative. Thus, for example, the "disciple whom Jesus loved" was left unnamed (John 13:23) to make it easy for each of us to slip into his place and be the beloved disciple, reclining next to Jesus at the Last Supper.

A further reason for the multiplicity of meanings in Scripture is a factor we have already considered. Many of the biblical books went through a long process of composition, even over centuries. Portions of the books acquired new meanings as they were assembled with other portions.

Take, for example, the accounts of Abraham and Sarah (Genesis 12–25). Their descendants handed on stories about this ancestor couple because the stories conveyed an assurance of God's presence with their family from generation to generation. At some point, the stories of Abraham and Sarah were combined with the accounts of creation and human rebellion against God that now appear in Genesis 1 to 11. Placed against the background of the breakdown in the relationship between God and the human race, God's dealings with Abraham and Sarah assume an additional meaning. They are seen to be part of a divine plan not only for their family but for the whole race. Against the background of creation and fall, God's promise of blessing to the couple appears as his first move toward remedying the alienation that had opened up between himself and all his human creatures. Thus through the editorial process the stories of Abraham and Sarah gained new meaning without losing their earlier meaning. We saw this process of accumulating meanings in the examples of editorial development described earlier (pages 41–45).

A further characteristic of the literal meaning of texts, both in the Bible and outside of it, is that what a person writes may contain more meaning than the person realizes. After the author has finished writing, other people may notice implications that he or she did not suspect; they may discern connections between the writer's words and the world that the writer had not noticed.

Take, for example, the American Declaration of Independence. The colonists declared that "all men are created equal" and are "endowed by their Creator" with "the right to ... liberty." This is a universal principle. It requires that every nation protect the basic rights of every member of society.

Yet the white, land-owning signers of the Declaration applied this universal principle in a less-than-universal way. They wished to stop the British government from violating *their* rights but were not especially concerned about the rights of men and women who were enslaved. Several of the signers of the Declaration, including its principal author, Thomas Jefferson, owned African-American slaves. These signers do not seem to have been fully conscious of what the principles in the Declaration meant for their slave-holding.

Within a few decades, however, other Americans came to view the Declaration of Independence as a mandate for the abolition of slavery. Their interpretation of the Declaration went beyond the authors' intention. But the abolitionists were not changing the meaning of the Declaration. On the contrary, they were more sensitive to the document's meaning than its authors had been. The abolitionists realized, as the Founding Fathers had not, that the universality of the Declaration—"all men are created equal"—removes any justification for slave-holding. It was the literal meaning that the abolitionists drew from the document, even though it went beyond the authors' intention.

Something similar to this occurred in the formation of the Old Testament. Based on their knowledge of God, the biblical authors expressed hopes for God's action. Eventually it became apparent that their writings pointed toward fullfillments greater than the authors realized.

For example, psalmists composed acclamations for Israelite kings that expressed a magnificent vision of kingship (Psalms 2, 45, 72). They envisioned a king who would give perfect justice to the poor and exercise sovereignty over the whole earth forever. No earthly king could attain this ideal, and it is difficult to know exactly what the psalmists themselves expected as they wrote these poetic words. Whatever their own thoughts, the psalmists' words expressed a meaning that exceeded anything they might have imagined. For in the mystery of his workings, God used their words to express his intention of establishing a king whose reign would more than fulfill the psalmists' hopes.

Quite possibly the psalmists would be surprised at the way God began to answer their prayers for his kingdom on earth through Jesus of Nazareth. Nevertheless, Jesus and the kingdom he brings are not a reversal of the psalmists' meaning. Jesus really is the one they celebrated when they wrote about God's establishing his rule on earth through an ideal king of Israel. God had guided them to write prayers that had more meaning than they realized.

This was often the case with the Old Testament authors. When, for example, they spoke of God's mercy and faithfulness and justice, their words pointed in the right direction, but toward fulfillments that were beyond their range of vision, over a horizon, so to speak.

The full meaning of the Old Testament writings began to come to light only with the coming of Jesus. He is the fulfillment of the expectations that God's words and deeds had aroused in Israel (Mark 12:10, 35-37; Luke 24:27). Jesus himself is the larger and deeper meaning of all God's actions reflected in the Old Testament.

In light of Jesus, many elements of the Old Testament are now seen to be foreshadowings, intimations, even prophecies of his saving death and resurrection. For example:

- Israel's escape at the Passover from slavery in Egypt is seen to be a demonstration of God's liberating power now brought to bear against sin and death through Jesus, the ultimate Passover lamb (1 Corinthians 5:7).

• Prophetic assurances that God would destroy the enemies of his people and reestablish the kingdom of Israel (Daniel 7) are seen to point not toward military conquest but toward Jesus' death and resurrection that has shattered the devil's dominion and opened the way for the coming of the Holy Spirit (John 12:31; Acts 1:4-8).

• The system of atonement through animal sacrifices mandated in the book of Leviticus is seen to be a prefigurement of the sacrificial death of Jesus, which perfectly bridges the gap between God and human beings (Hebrews 5, 7–10).

• The prophets' hope that the scattered people of Israel would be gathered to worship God in a glorious Jerusalem temple (Ezekiel 40-47) is seen to be a veiled reference to the community of Jesus' followers, who will ultimately be gathered into eternal life with him (Revelation 4–5, 21).

Thus the Old Testament writings have two related levels of meaning. There is the level of literal meaning—what the authors sought to communicate to the readers of their own times. And there is the level of meaning at which the text points toward Jesus' death and resurrection.

This second level is called the *spiritual* meaning. The spiritual meaning of the Old Testament books is their meaning within the whole divine plan of salvation. We might say that it is the meaning of the Old Testament seen from God's point of view. His angle of vision on the Old Testament is opened up to us by Jesus and by the New Testament writers through the action of the Holy Spirit—which is the essential reason this meaning is called "spiritual."

Jesus' accomplishment exceeds the thinking of the Old Testament authors. He fulfilled God's plan at a level above their expectations. Thus the spiritual meaning of the Old Testament writings goes beyond the authors' intentions. Even so, this new range of meaning in their words is not a reversal of the meaning they intended. There is no break in continuity between the literal meaning of the Old Testament authors and the meaning of their words as pointers toward Jesus. They speak of God's mercy, justice, faithfulness, and forgiveness in terms accessible to their listeners. God displayed this same mercy, justice, faithfulness, and forgiveness perfectly in the life, death, and resurrection of his Son.

In Jesus, God brought to fulfillment the plan that he had been pursuing in the history of Israel and that is reflected, in fragmentary ways, in the Old Testament. The events narrated in the Old Testament— God's covenant with Abraham, the exodus from Egypt, Israel's possession of the land of Canaan, and so on—belonged to the one stream of divine activity that was flowing toward Jesus. In Old Testament events, God was preparing for and prefiguring the coming of his Son. Thus the spiritual meaning of the Old Testament writings grows out of their literal meaning as flower from seed. As Jesus declared, the biblical books had pointed to him all along (John 5:39-47).

What is the relationship between the New Testament and the spiritual meaning? The spiritual meaning is what the text means in relation to Jesus' death and resurrection. Since the New Testament writers view everything in light of Jesus' death and resurrection, in the New Testament the literal meaning *is* the spiritual meaning.

Literal and Spiritual Meanings

This book uses the terms "literal meaning" and "spiritual meaning" in the way which the Pontifical Biblical Commission currently employs these terms. Over the centuries, these terms have been used in somewhat different ways. Another, somewhat different but quite common, way of speaking about the different meanings of Scripture is expressed in a medieval Latin jingle that might be translated:

The literal meaning teaches what was done.
The allegorical meaning, what you should believe.
The moral meaning, what you should do.
The anagogical meaning, where you should be heading.

This division of meanings, or "senses," brings out the richness of Scripture. The *allegorical* (sometimes called *typological*) meaning designates the way that realities in the Old Testament function as signs of Christ and sacramental life. The *moral* refers to the way in which scriptural persons and events offer lessons about how we should live (sometimes it is called the *tropological* meaning, from a Greek word meaning "figurative"). The *anagogical* meaning (from the Greek for "leading upward") refers to realities and events in the Bible that stand as images of our final fulfillment in Christ. For example, in Scripture the city of Jerusalem represents the gathering of God's people in the new creation. For more on these levels of meaning, and other explanations of how Scripture communicates its message, see the *Catechism of the Catholic Church*, sections 101–133.

Discovering the Literal Meaning

How do we discover Scripture's literal and spiritual meanings? Let's begin with the literal meanings of Scripture. A statement by the bishops at Vatican Council II helpfully sets the agenda for discovering the literal meanings:

> In determining the intention of the sacred writers, attention must be paid ... to "literary forms, for the fact is that truth is differently presented and expressed in the various types of historical writing, in prophetical and poetical texts," and in other forms of literary expression. Hence the exegete must look for that meaning which the sacred writer, in a determined situation and given the circumstances of his time and culture, intended to express and did in fact express, through the medium of a contemporary literary form. Rightly to understand what the sacred author wanted to affirm in his work, due attention must be paid both to the customary and characteristic patterns of perception, speech, and narrative which prevailed at the age of the sacred writer, and to the conventions which the people of his time followed in their dealings with one another.[4]

In this instruction, the bishops direct our attention to four areas that we need to consider if we are to grasp the authors' intended meanings.

1. Type of writing, or, as the bishops put it, "literary forms."
The bishops write that, "'truth is differently presented and expressed in the various types of historical writing, in prophetical and poetical texts,' and in other forms of literary expression." We are all

familiar with this principle. To understand what we read—or hear or view—we need to know what *kind* of communication we are receiving. We would reach dangerous conclusions if we took the computer-generated fantasies of a car commercial as a guide for how to drive (it's not a training video) or if we made decisions about cancer treatment from what we saw in a TV soap opera about doctors (it's not a documentary).

The biblical library contains various types of writing (sometimes called *genres*). We must take account of them if we are to understand what we are reading. A poem "means" differently from a letter, a parable differently from a history.

Since the Bible was composed in cultural settings quite different from ours, some of its types of writing are unfamiliar to us. Mythological tales, tribal traditions, prophecies—these types of writing do not belong to our modern cultural vocabulary. They may be as puzzling to us as a car commercial would be to a person who lived back then. The biblical library also contains types of writing that are familiar to us—memoirs, genealogies, essays—but often in forms different from ours.

Learning how the various kinds of biblical writing "work" is important for understanding what the authors were saying. For example, the long section of the book of Exodus that stretches from 20:1 to 24:8 is an adaptation of an ancient covenant formula. Knowing something about the structure of ancient Near Eastern covenants can help us focus on the main points in this lengthy section and not get lost in the mass of legal details.

By the same token, awareness of the types of material in the Bible helps us avoid misunderstanding. Familiarity with the nature of apocalyptic writing can guard us from reading the books of Daniel or Revelation as coded descriptions of specific twenty-first-century events. As we have seen, we can avoid useless conflicts over the early chapters of Genesis if we understand what kinds of writing they do and do not contain(pages 52–54).

2. Background. The bishops speak of the importance of knowing about the "circumstances" of the biblical writer's "time and culture."

Consider these questions: Is a dollar tip generous or stingy? Is a question about a person's ethnic identity a discriminatory act? Obviously it all depends. To answer these questions you have to know whether the tip-leaver just ate a piece of pie or a five-course meal, whether the questioner was a census taker or a loan officer in a bank. In addition to this kind of "foreground" information, you also need some background information. In what situations is tipping expected, and what is the normal rate? Why would a census taker or a banker be asking questions about a person's ethnicity?

Writers often give foreground information but say little or nothing about background, counting on their readers' familiarity with it. This creates a problem when writer and reader come from different cultures. If the writer has assumed that the reader knows about etiquette, monetary values, patterns of courtship, religious ceremonies, business practices, class structures, and so on, the reader who is unfamiliar with such background may have a hard time following the story. This, of course, is often our situation in reading the Bible.

For instance, it is difficult to understand the story of Jacob (Genesis 25–36) unless we know something about patterns of inheritance, shepherding practices, and marriage contracts in the ancient Near East. In the book of Ruth, what is so significant about Ruth's being a Moabite (Ruth 1:1-4)? Why in Proverbs 31:23 does the author make a point of saying that the man who is married to Lady Wisdom "is known at the city gates"? We need background! We need to understand the things that the biblical authors assumed as they wrote for people in their own cultures.

In many cases we will miss some of the meaning if we are not able to view a biblical passage against its cultural background. For example, ancient Near Eastern peoples conceived of creation as the outcome of a struggle between gods. Mesopotamian stories pictured a god vanquishing a divine ocean-monster and dividing her up to form the world. In Genesis, by contrast, God creates not by conflict but simply by command. The sea is merely part of God's creation; sea beasts are elements of the ecosystem, not divine powers. Thus the Genesis account shows that God had no need to compete with any other deities in order to bring the universe into existence. God holds absolute sovereignty and exercises limitless creative power. But this message emerges clearly only when we compare the Genesis account to the creation stories of Israel's polytheistic neighbors.

Often what the biblical writers do *not* say is as important as what they do say. But only if we are acquainted with their culture will we be able to "hear" the silence. For example, some of the psalms are prayers for healing (Psalms 6, 22, 31). To an extent, they resemble the prayers of the Israelites' pagan neighbors to their various gods. But the Israelites' psalms lack something present in many of their neighbors' prayers: incantations against evil spirits. The Israelites did share their neighbors' belief that evil spirits can inflict sicknesses, but they did not use magical formulas to drive them out. Rather, they simply asked God for healing. The absence of magic in the psalms expresses the Israelites' trust in God's mercy, faithfulness, and power.

Like ignorance of type of writing, ignorance of background can lead to misunderstandings. The author of the Gospel of John often refers to Jesus' opponents as "the Jews" (John 5:15-18; 7:1; 9:18). The reader who does not understand the first-century religious situation may mistakenly think that John is condemning Judaism.

3. Situation and purpose. The bishops teach that the interpreter of Scripture "must look for that meaning which the sacred writer, in a determined situation," that is, in a particular situation, "intended to express." Each biblical author was communicating to particular people in a particular situation. If we wish to know what he said to them, it helps a lot to know about the recipients for whom the author shaped his communication and the reasons he had for writing to them.

Someone has said that interpretation is the art of reading texts so that their own concerns are understood. The writers of the biblical books were dealing with concerns that were to some degree different from ours. We need to grasp their concerns if we are to perceive their meaning.

Hosea prophesied, "I desire steadfast love and not sacrifice" (Hosea 6:6). Was that a declaration that God wanted the Jewish sacrificial system dismantled? Paul criticized the Christians in Galatia for wanting to observe "special days, and months, and seasons" (Galatians 4:10). Was he ruling out an annual liturgical cycle? You might think so, if you did not know something about the situations they were dealing with.

Actually, Hosea and Paul were combating distorted views of how people should relate to God. Their words were verbal attacks on mistaken notions. But an attack rarely provides a well-rounded treatment of a subject. When we recognize Hosea's and Paul's purposes, we will not take their words as comprehensive statements about the place of religious practices in our relationship with God.

Since the prophets constantly addressed particular social and political issues, whole sections of the prophetic books become comprehensible—and interesting—only when we have some idea of the situations they were dealing with. Many of the New Testament letters were written to counter false understandings of the gospel. Failing to consider what those false views were, some commentators have arrived at flawed interpretations.

A case in point is Paul's words in his letter to the Galatians criticizing "works of the law" (3:10). In writing to the Galatians, Paul was rejecting the view that Gentile Christians must become Jews and follow the entire Mosaic law. By dismissing "works of the law," he was rejecting his opponents' emphasis on certain Jewish religious practices. The apostle was not indiscriminately criticizing all religious practices. He was certainly not asserting that our cooperation with God's grace plays no part in our salvation. Through a failure to grasp the concerns that Paul was dealing with in his letter, his words against "works of the law" have sometimes been misapplied as an argument against the Catholic sacramental system and against the Catholic teaching of the importance of our human cooperation with God's grace.

On the positive side, learning about the situation the biblical author is addressing can open our eyes to the central message of a biblical book. For example, the Book of Revelation comes into clearer focus when we understand the social pressures to compromise their faith that faced the Christians to whom John addressed the book.

4. Structure. "Attention must be paid to the customary and characteristic patterns of perception, speech, and narrative which prevailed at the age of the sacred writer," the bishops write. In other words, we need to understand how people in the ancient cultures of biblical times expressed themselves in writing.

Ancient writers fashioned their works in shapes and patterns unfamiliar to us. Without some sense of how they arranged their poetry and ordered their historical narratives, we will miss some of the beauty and meaning of the biblical writings.

For example, ancient Semitic writers were fond of bringing a section of writing to an end by returning to a word or idea used at the beginning (thus creating what is called an *inclusion*). This return provided a sense of closure and had the practical advantage of marking the end of a section. In those days, books did not have chapter divisions or subheadings or even paragraph indentations to show where one section ended and another began.

Noticing a pattern of inclusion can help us see how a writer has divided up his material into units. This, in turn, helps us follow his train of thought. A couple of examples of inclusion may be found in the Gospel of John: chapter 14, verses 1 to 3 are echoed in verses 27 to 31; in chapter 21, verse 1 is echoed in verse 14.

The Gospel of Luke provides another example of how the structure of a book helps to express its meaning. Luke has arranged his account of Jesus' public life in such a way that Jesus leaves Galilee for Jerusalem in chapter 9—rather early in Luke's account of his public life. As a result, Jesus does much of his teaching and interacting with people as he is on the road to Jerusalem, the city where he will die (Luke 10–18). By arranging his narrative this way, Luke indicates that being a disciple of Jesus means being on the road with him, hanging loose from worldly investments in order to stay close to him.

The Help We Need

One practical consequence of these considerations is quite simple. To discover the biblical authors' meanings, we need some expert assistance.

We need, first of all, the kind of help that biblical scholars call the *historical-critical method.* Here "critical" does not mean "negative"; it means proceeding according to defined methods and criteria of investigation. Employing historical criticism, scholars illuminate both the historical background behind the biblical books and the history of their composition—how oral traditions arose, how documents were written, how material was assembled and edited together and revised. For this, scholars draw on studies into ancient languages and information about ancient cultures and events derived from archaeology, from nonbiblical writings, and from other kinds of evidence.

Looking at the Bible from a different viewpoint, other scholars help us understand the biblical books as finished writings. Their work is sometimes called *literary criticism.* Having become familiar with the literature of the ancient world, these scholars help us understand the structures of the biblical books and the artistry by which they achieve their purposes of instructing and encouraging us.

Such scholarly expertise aids us in understanding the literal meaning of the biblical writings. This is why modern popes, especially Pius XII and John Paul II, have made it clear that these forms of scholarly help are indispensable for interpreting the Bible.

Now, it must be acknowledged that there have been problems with modern biblical scholarship. The Pontifical Biblical Commission, an advisory body of Catholic scholars selected by the Holy See, pointed out several deficiencies in an analysis in 1993 entitled *The Interpretation of the Bible in the Church:*

- Scholars sometimes treat Scripture as though it were merely an ancient document, part of a world that has passed away. The Bible then seems separated from the present by an unbridgeable gulf of centuries, unable to speak to us today.

- Historical methods that illuminate the stages of writing and editing of the Bible may put such a heavy emphasis on the human dimension of the text that there is a danger the divine author will be overlooked.

- Methods that dissect the biblical writings in a search for the pieces from which they were composed may leave Scripture in pieces. The sense of a whole, of a unified message, may be lost.

- In an effort to be impartial, some scholars set faith to one side.

- The tools of scholarly study may be employed for partisan purposes. For example, scholarship has sometimes been used to attack the Church by attempting to demonstrate that the biblical writings, on which the Church bases its faith and practice, are full of distortions. Theories about the development of the early Church have been used to dismiss the New Testament writings as historically unreliable.

The Church has needed to defend the faith against such problems in scholarship. Indeed, in the late nineteenth century Pope Leo XIII encouraged Catholic biblical scholarship mainly as a defense against such problems. Popes after him called on Catholic scholars to guard against importing into their work views that are alien to Christian tradition; for example, to be on guard against the view that miracles must be attributable to merely natural causes or that Jesus did not intend to establish a Church.

Yet from Pope Pius XII in 1943 to the present, popes have also promoted biblical scholarship because of its inherent value for the Church. In a statement in 1993, John Paul II pointed out that the historical-critical method, freed from philosophical presuppositions contrary to truth and faith, is the starting point for understanding Scripture, since it is the starting point for grasping the human authors' meanings.[5]

In recent years some Catholics have wanted to leave modern biblical scholarship aside and return to the interpretations of the Church

Fathers of the first Christian centuries, such as St. John Chrysostom and St. Augustine. Modern Church leaders have certainly encouraged interest in the Fathers. In their homilies and commentaries on Scripture, the Fathers read Scripture with great spiritual sensitivity, in a way that makes them a model for every age. The Fathers' comments on Scripture are marked by depth, pastoral concern, hunger for God, appreciation of the mystery of Christ.

Nevertheless, the Fathers' interpretive approach has deficiencies. The Fathers had little sense of the human authors as authors or of the historical development of tradition in the Bible. Often the Fathers

> The sacred Synod encourages those sons of the Church who are biblical scholars to continue energetically with the work they have so well begun, with a constant renewal of vigor and with loyalty to the mind of the Church.
> *Dogmatic Constitution on Divine Revelation* (23)[6]

offered allegorical explanations that seem distant from the meaning of the human authors of Scripture. In many cases, the Fathers' knowledge of the historical setting and the languages of the Bible, especially Hebrew and Aramaic, was rather limited.

The Fathers themselves did not think they had spoken the last interpretive words on the Bible. They were very much aware of unfathomed depths in Scripture—and of their own limitations. St. Augustine, for example, wrote a commentary on Genesis, then went back and wrote another—and another, because he felt that he had not adequately dealt with the issues in the book. It would not have surprised the Fathers that later scholars might shed new light on the Bible. Authors such as St. Jerome and St. Augustine often declare their openness to someone offering a better interpretation than their own.

In the last couple of centuries, scholars working in various fields have learned an enormous amount about the ancient Near Eastern and Mediterranean worlds where the Bible was written. Through modern linguistic, historical, cultural, and literary research, aspects of the Bible have become accessible in new ways. As the Pontifical Biblical Commission declared, modern studies have "made it possible to understand far more accurately the intention of the authors and editors of the Bible, as well as the message which they addressed to their first readers."[7]

In the pursuit of the truth communicated to us in Scripture, we would be mistaken to ignore these tools for understanding. To do so would not be safer; it would be anti-intellectual. Quoting Leo XIII, Pope John Paul II has encouraged biblical scholars to "be alert to adopt without delay anything useful that each period brings to biblical exegesis."[8] Pius XII reminded those who regarded modern biblical scholarship as a threat that not everything new is to be feared![9]

On balance, we need both older and newer approaches to the Bible. The historical-critical method, while not enough by itself, is necessary, as the Pontifical Biblical Commission has argued. The same is true of the interpretations of the Fathers and other writers of the past. To plumb the depths of Scripture, we need both the Fathers and the modern scholars. The wise reader will draw from both the old and the new (Matthew 13:52).

Discovering the Spiritual Meaning

In a famous line, St. Augustine wrote that the New Testament is concealed in the Old and the Old Testament is made manifest in the New. While the spiritual meaning of the Old Testament is not contrary to the literal meaning, it is hidden, because God's plan of salvation in Christ was a divine secret (Ephesians 1:7-10). A measure of the hiddenness of the Old Testament's spiritual meaning is the surprise of Jesus' contemporaries, including his disciples, when he began to reveal it.

Although the spiritual meaning of the Old Testament is hidden, it is not subjective or imaginary. It is a meaning that God has placed there. As Pope John Paul II pointed out, not just *any* spiritual interpretation can be attributed to the biblical text. In determining the spiritual sense, "a merely subjective inspiration is insufficient. One must be able to show that it is a sense 'willed by God himself,' a spiritual meaning 'given by God' to the inspired text. Determining the spiritual sense then belongs itself to the realm of exegetical science."[10] In other words, discovering the spiritual meaning, like discovering the literal meaning, requires scholarly, theological investigation.

What principles enable us to discover the true spiritual meaning of the Old Testament? The Pontifical Biblical Commission says that the spiritual meaning of Scripture is "the meaning expressed by the biblical texts when read under the influence of the Holy Spirit, in the contexts of the paschal mystery of Christ and of the new life which flows from it."[11] This suggests that the primary source of guidance for perceiving the spiritual meaning of the Old Testament is the New Testament, since the New Testament is the authoritative witness to the mystery of Christ. In the Gospels and the other New Testament writings, first Jesus himself and then the New Testament authors explain the spiritual meaning of various portions of the Old Testament. These explanations are our primary guide to its spiritual meaning.

With the help of the Holy Spirit, the Church's understanding of the spiritual meaning of the Old Testament has grown since the New Testament was written. The Spirit's influence can be seen especially in the writings of the Church Fathers, especially on the points where they tend to agree. An example would be the early Christian writers' growing understanding of Adam as a prefigurement of Christ.

The Spirit's guidance is also reflected in the Church's liturgical life. Thus the ways that the Eucharistic liturgy and the sacraments take up texts of the Old Testament and apply them to Christ and Christian life is a trustworthy indicator of the texts' spiritual meaning.

In an attempt to unearth the spiritual meanings in the Old Testament, Christians ever since Clement of Alexandria in the second century have proposed many allegorical interpretations. Teachers have used allegorical interpretation to show how everything from the number of Jacob's sons in Genesis to the appearance of the beloved's teeth in the Song of Songs speak about Christ and Christian life. To what extent can we take this approach as a guide for discovering the spiritual meaning of the Bible?

St. Augustine and St. Thomas Aquinas allowed for great freedom of interpretation. So long as the reader stayed within the bounds of the teaching of the Church and the rule of charity, any interpretation might be entertained. Nevertheless, some allegorical interpretations offered by writers of the past seem today to be projections of readers' thoughts into the text rather than discoveries drawn out of it.

Celestin Charlier wrote that the Fathers emphasized the fundamental themes of Christian faith, "but in the margin they devised a whole mass of flourishes, variations, and improvisations which could be called semi-poetic flights of fancy."[12] Over the centuries, some of the allegorizing, by both notable saints and obscure thinkers, has been somewhat fanciful. In the modern period, Church leaders have expressed caution about this approach to discovering the spiritual meaning of Scripture. Pope Pius XII warned preachers against substituting allegorizing for interpretation that brings out the meaning of the inspired authors. People want to know what the biblical authors had to say, Pope Pius observed, not what a clever preacher is capable of imagining.[13]

It should be noted that the Fathers and later writers who used the Old Testament in an allegorical way did not necessarily assert that they were drawing out meanings from the text. Often they were simply employing biblical imagery and events as the language in which to discuss God, prayer, spiritual life, and so on.

Imaginative, even playful uses of Scripture are sometimes helpful in order to give details in the Bible an application to our lives. They may aid us in private meditation and reflection. But in our search to understand the spiritual meaning of the Old Testament, we will do well to be guided by the main sources of interpretation—the New Testament, the Fathers, the liturgy.

Celestin Charlier suggests that the spiritual meaning of the Old Testament is better seen in the larger themes and developments in the Bible than in single words or details. For example, Charlier argues, what makes Joshua spiritually a prefigurement of Jesus is not his name (which in the Hebrew is the same as "Jesus") but his role as the one who secures the land for God's people.[14]

Chapter Eight

How Can It Speak to Me?
The Bible in Your Life

In the Byzantine liturgy, before the people go forward to receive Communion, the priest holds out the chalice and intones: "Approach with fear of God and with faith." These words might suitably sound in our ears as we open the Bible. In the Bible also, Jesus, the living Word of God, comes to us. Reading the Bible, like receiving Communion, is a response to his personal love for us. We do well to approach with "fear of God" and "faith."

> The Church has always venerated the divine Scriptures just as she has venerated the Body of the Lord.
> *Dogmatic Constitution on Divine Revelation* (21)[1]

Fear of God means reverence and awe, not cringing timidity or anxiety about punishment. Reverence is appropriate when we read the Bible because in its words we encounter God, who is mystery beyond comprehension. In the words of human authors and editors, the God who created us speaks to us. That *is* awesome!

Fear of God also means obeying and trusting in him (Genesis 22:12). God being the creator, and we being creatures, there is no place for distrust and unwillingness to obey in our relationship with him. It is difficult to surrender ourselves to God, but the biblical writers encourage us with the counsel that "the fear of the Lord is the beginning of wisdom" (Proverbs 9:10; see Job 28:28; Psalm 111:10; Sirach 1:16).

Deciding to put our lives in God's hands and cooperate with him is the starting point for hearing his words to us in the Bible, because true hearing is obeying. In the Bible itself, the word "hear" often serves to mean "hear and obey" (Deuteronomy 4:1, NAB). If we wish to truly hear God as we open the Bible, we must begin with willingness to respond to what we will find there.

As to faith, the key to reading the Bible as God's word to you is to *believe* that it is God's word to you. This belief is well founded. God continues to unfold the plan of salvation recounted in the Bible and calls each of us to participate in it. He has a role for you and me to play. The words recorded in Scripture that he spoke to those who took part in earlier stages of his plan, are now his words to us, who are invited to participate in a later stage of his plan.

Faith that God will speak to us as we read the Bible is grounded in the presence of the Holy Spirit. The Spirit moved the men and women of the old covenant to hear and respond to God's words. Through the Spirit, the Son took flesh and carried out his ministry. After his resurrection the Son gave the Spirit to the community of his followers. This Spirit now makes us the living body of Christ. In the worship of the Church, the Spirit transforms the bread and wine of the Eucharistic offering into the living Christ. As we read the Bible, the same Spirit brings its words to life for us.

Scripture is an inspired and inspiring word. Just as God inspired the Bible's authors as they wrote, so he wishes to inspire us as we read. Of course, this does not mean that we will have a distinct sense of God's guidance or an unusual experience of his love every time we read the Bible. It is doubtful that the biblical authors themselves had any special spiritual experience as they wrote. Our reading of the Bible is an ordinary human experience, as the writing seems to have been an ordinary human experience. But just as God worked through the authors' praying, thinking, and writing, so he will work through our reading, studying, pondering, and praying. Bible reading, like the Bible itself, is a divine-human phenomenon. As we read the Bible, God works through the human abilities he has given us, accomplishing things that go far beyond human abilities. The Spirit leads us to know and love God.

If we come to Scripture with "fear of God and faith," God will reveal himself to us. The process involves desire on our part, patience in letting God reveal himself however he chooses, and readiness to respond when he does. "Blessed are the pure in heart, for they will see God" (Matthew 5:8).

Just Read It!

After all the explanations of the preceding chapters, we arrive at a simple, practical point regarding the Bible: We need to read it! And, since we have a daily need to hear God's word, we need to read the Bible daily. The Bible is deep and broad, and sometimes difficult, and only through regular reading will we be able to gradually grow in understanding it. Quite simply, the most important decision you can make regarding the Bible is to make it part of your daily routine.

Are you willing to give the Bible priority amid the other pressing matters in your life? The psalmist appeals to us, "O that today you would listen to his voice! Do not harden your hearts" (Psalm 95:7-8). The first question this exhortation raises is not "Will you harden your heart against God's voice?" but simply "Will you notice that he is speaking to you?" God wishes to communicate with you. Will you take the time to pay attention?

This question needs a very specific answer—an answer that specifies a particular time and a particular place. Exactly when and where will you read the Bible today—and tomorrow? Each of us needs to find one time and place that will work for us regularly. What is this time and place for you?

I suggest aiming for fifteen to twenty minutes of Bible reading a day. Less than this is too little to collect your thoughts and make any progress. More than this may go beyond what you can squeeze into a busy life. Better to make a realistic commitment and stick with it than fail in the attempt to reach a higher goal.

With reading the Bible, as with learning a foreign language, better a little every day than a longer period less frequently. Somewhere, somehow, just about every one of us can find fifteen to twenty minutes each day to read the Bible. With determination and God's help, we can stay with it.

The goal in our daily reading is not to read as much as possible but to understand and digest what we read. Thus we need to read carefully and thoughtfully. This means adopting a slower pace than we use in scanning a newspaper or racing through a novel.

Reading the Bible is more like walking down a street than driving on an expressway. Read a section through, then read it again more slowly, asking questions. Pause. Linger. Bible reading, George Martin has written, is "leisurely reading, reading with attention to detail."[2]

Growing in Understanding

From our earlier chapters, it should be apparent that every one of us needs help to understand the Bible. Help is not something that only the exceptionally ignorant need; it is not something we can outgrow. Reading the Bible with help is normal.

Obviously, as Raymond Brown once remarked, "God can speak to the reader without the permission of scholars."[3] But to gain an accurate and in-depth understanding, we need the support of scholars, saints, and other teachers past and present. Reading the Bible is like going on a guided tour. You go in order to see for yourself, but you go with a guide because you need help to understand what you see.

We read the Bible as members of the community of the Bible, the Church. This is true even when we read the Bible in solitude. When we read alone, other members of the community can nonetheless be present with us through their written words—in the introductions and notes in our Bible, in commentaries, in devotional guides and other sorts of help. These resources enable us to read the Bible within the faith and understanding of the Church.

All this means that reading the Bible involves a study component. Study, of course, requires effort—an effort at which we may chafe. We tend to want Scripture to be simple because we want our relationship with God to be simple. At root, both are in fact simple. But then, both are also complex. The events through which God has acted in history are complex. The world and we ourselves are endlessly complex. It would be unreasonable to expect that the Bible would not also be complex. In life, growing in understanding and maturity is a long, difficult process. Similarly, a long process stretches before us as we seek to understand and respond to God's word in Scripture.

To think that the Spirit will override the complexities and give us infused knowledge as we sit by ourselves with a Bible without any notes or other study aids is a kind of superspiritualism—expecting God to circumvent the natural processes that he has created. He has given us minds because he wants us to use them. The biblical authors had to observe, think, pray, write, edit. We, too, have to make some effort if we are to understand and profit from their words. God did not

> As seekers, we cannot just skim the surface, amassing bits of unconnected information. Despite promises we often hear, there is no instant wisdom. Genuine wisdom requires the patient process of seeing the connections between facts and relating them to form the bigger picture. Bible literacy is measured by assimilation, not accumulation.
>
> Steve Mueller[4]

simply dictate the Bible to the human authors; he does not simply unveil the mysteries in Scripture to readers who are unwilling to use their ordinary human capacities to learn.

While we need to study, we do not need to become scholars. True, the Bible has depths that will keep us learning and growing for a lifetime. But it was not written for academics or geniuses. The Bible was written for ordinary people, and with modest help all of us can read it with understanding.

Bible teacher Steve Mueller has observed that "the most common fear when approaching the formidable journey of Bible reading is that we are not smart enough."[5] But we are. Mueller adds, "You don't have to become an expert on the Bible, but you do need to become a more competent reader." That is a realizable goal for all of us.

As we begin to read the Bible, we discover a lot we do not understand—and we continue to have this experience no matter how much we learn. After years of reading, my knowledge of the Bible seems like a few small islands of understanding in an ocean of ignorance. This can be unnerving or discouraging, but it need not be.

We should focus on what we do understand and not be disturbed by all that we do not. If we take a gradual, persevering approach to learning, our islands of knowledge will grow at least into a modest atoll.

While some of the Bible is hard to understand, other parts are actually easy to understand but hard to respond to. It is not hard to see what Jesus is driving at when he says to love those who do us harm (Luke 6:27-36), but it is exceedingly difficult to put this into practice. No matter how slowly our comprehension of Scripture grows, there will always be plenty of parts that we already understand well enough but have not yet fully applied to our lives. No one ever gets to the point where he or she could say, "I've put into practice everything in Scripture that I understand. I would be willing to apply more of it to my life, if only I could understand it!"

Responding to what we understand in the Bible is a crucial part of growing in understanding. Some of what we do not grasp in the Bible is obscure to us because our worldliness and selfishness keep us from comprehending the message of God's love and his call to love others that lies at the center of the Bible. The scholars on the Pontifical Biblical Commission observe that "as the reader matures in the life of the Spirit, there grows also his or her capacity to understand the realities of which the Bible speaks."[6] As we grow in love, the Bible becomes more transparent to us.

What Does It Mean for Me?

Obviously, study is not the be-all and end-all of our relationship with the Bible. We study so that we may understand. We seek to understand so that we may live the lives God calls us to live and attain the goal God has created us to enjoy. Thus, as we gain some idea of what a portion of Scripture means, we naturally go on to ponder what it means for us.

The basic question that constantly confronts us in reading the Bible is how what we are reading affects our lives here and now. Occasionally the answer will leap from the text and address us so clearly and directly it will seem that God has written the passage just for us. More often, we will need to do some thinking in order to discover the connections between the biblical text and ourselves. God will speak to us through the Bible not only in the moments of sudden, powerful insight, but also imperceptibly in the process of reflection.

Various questions can help us find points of contact between the biblical text and our twenty-first-century lives. We can ask ourselves:

> One of the great thrills of reading the Bible ... is the recognition that the biblical situation is similar to our own. What God demanded by way of response in times past, he is still demanding today.
>
> Raymond E. Brown, S.S.[7]

When have I experienced something like what the people in the text experienced? How does my experience help me understand their thoughts and feelings? What aspect of my life do these words of the Bible lead me to examine? (The text speaks of forgiveness. Whom have I failed to forgive?) How does this passage of Scripture cause me to evaluate an aspect of my life? What can I learn from the way people in this passage responded, or failed to respond, to God?

We can try to put ourselves into the text. One way to do this is to recreate the scene in our imagination, place ourselves within it, and then observe what takes place. We can ask: How does it affect me? How am I inclined to act in the situation? What do I wish to say to the Lord?

Another approach is to identify with a participant in the narrative. For example, consider the parable of the father with two sons (Luke

15:11-32). Reading the parable, we may realize we are like the son who rejects his father. We ask ourselves, then: What do the father's words to him say to me? Then we think: The son who stays home with the father but is angry at him—that's me too! How do the father's words to him speak to me? And the father who is patient with both his wayward sons—that also is me! Whose weaknesses am I called to be patient with?[8]

Some people find it useful to explore questions such as these over a period of time by keeping a journal. Some find that discussion of the Bible with other people is helpful for digging out its implications for life today. When we hear how other people are hearing God's word to them in the Bible, we are helped to see how he is speaking to us also.

> *Te totum applica ad textum. Rem totam applica ad te.* Apply your whole self to the text. Apply the whole text to yourself.
>
> J.A. Bengel

Pray

Bible reading is an opportunity for encounter with God. "In the sacred books the Father who is in heaven lovingly comes to meet his children and talks with them," the bishops at Vatican Council II wrote. Thus, the bishops insisted, prayer should accompany our reading of the Bible, "so that there might be a conversation between God and man."[9]

We need the guidance of the Church, the assistance of scholars, the support of one another to understand the Bible and to see how it applies to our lives. But as we read his word, each of us has the responsibility to seek God. No one can meet God for us.

Prayer emerges from Bible reading by a natural process. It is only because God has already acted toward us that we can make any response to him. Thus, prayer begins with listening to God and perceiving what he has done for us. And this, of course, is exactly where the Bible puts the accent. It speaks of God's action. It places everything we do in the frame of God's initiative.

Thus every passage of Scripture issues a call to conversion. Conversion, turning back to God, arises from our recognition that the saving events described in the Bible are *for us*. Scripture reminds us that God gives us life today, calls us and makes promises to us today, rescues us and comes to us today.

Prayer, then, weaves naturally in and out of Bible reading, study, and reflection. There is no formula for praying Scripture, for there is no formula for praying. Prayer is conversation with God, and the essence of the conversation lies not in words but in an interaction at a deeper level—in attentiveness, trust, love. In prayer, heart speaks to heart.

Scripture leads us to an encounter with God in a multitude of ways. The Bible can awe us with the breadth and depth of God's love for the human race. It can shatter our independence and pride with a single word of reproach. It provides us with prayers for our use—psalms and numerous other prayers and hymns throughout the Old and New Testaments. We are invited to meditate on the truths God reveals, to ruminate on particular words and phrases, to recreate in our imagination the scenes that are described, to sit in silent wonder, to thank, to praise.

The most profound praying of Scripture takes place in the celebration of the Eucharist. The Bible bears witness to God's saving deeds in history; in the Eucharistic liturgy we most solemnly remember God's deeds in an act of public thanksgiving. In the Eucharist, as we recall the climax of God's saving deeds in Jesus' death and resurrection, this mystery becomes present anew.

In the Eucharist, we enter into the realities at the heart of the Bible. We are caught up in Jesus' offering of himself to the Father by which he has reconciled us to God and restored our relationship with God lost through sin. We join the saints and angels in the heavenly liturgy of praise they offer to God for all eternity. We eat the bread of eternal life—Jesus' life-giving body and blood—and experience a foretaste of the banquet that he will share with us in the kingdom of God.

Thus in the Eucharist we experience the divine life toward which all of Scripture points. The Eucharist brings us into communion with the Lord of Scripture and provides us with the most profound opportunity to express to him our gratitude for his love.

Whoever thinks that he understands the divine Scriptures or any part of them so that it does not build the double love of God and of our neighbor does not understand it at all.

St. Augustine, *On Christian Doctrine,* 1:36

Chapter Nine

Where Do I Start?
Buying a Bible and Finding Your Way Around in It

To read the Bible, you must have a Bible. There are many different translations and editions available. How can you choose among them? Our discussion so far suggests the following criteria for the kind of Bible you should get.

- *A Bible with all its parts.* Select a version that contains all the Old Testament books recognized by the Catholic Church (see pages 85–87). Every version prepared under Catholic auspices has the entire Catholic Old Testament; some versions prepared under Protestant and ecumenical auspices do too. Check the table of contents against the listing of Old Testament books on page 14.

- *A version in harmony with the Church.* In order to read the Bible with the Church, select one that bears an "imprimatur" (a Latin word meaning "it may be printed") on the copyright page. This indicates that a Catholic bishop has determined that nothing in the translation, introductions, or notes conflicts with the Church's teaching. All versions prepared under Catholic auspices have an imprimatur; so also do some editions prepared under Protestant and ecumenical auspices.

- *A study Bible.* I hope the preceding chapters have persuaded you that we all need help to read the Bible with understanding. A convenient form for that help is a study Bible. A study Bible contains introductory articles, notes at the bottom or in the margins of pages, maps, and other resources.

  A study Bible is different from a "reader's edition," which supplies few or no notes, and from a "devotional" Bible, which incorporates material to help you to pray and apply the Bible to your life but does not shed much light on the meaning of the text. At Vatican II, the bishops wrote that Catholic scholars and publishers ought to produce versions of the Bible "furnished with necessary and truly adequate explanations," so that Catholics can become "familiar with the sacred Scriptures and steeped in their spirit."[1] That describes a study Bible.

- *A modern translation.* The Bible is sometimes difficult to understand. We don't need translations that add to our difficulties. Rather, we need translations that employ all available scholarly resources to put the Hebrew, Aramaic, and Greek texts of Scripture into clear, comprehensible English. Older translations have their value, but for various reasons are not the easiest to understand (and they have other shortcomings also; see box, page 135–36).

Put these four criteria together, and where does that leave you? To be honest, without a lot of options. While there are several modern translations that contain the entire Catholic Old Testament and are approved for Catholic use, I know of only two adult study Bibles. They are *The Catholic Study Bible* and *The Catholic Bible: Personal Study Edition,* both published by Oxford University Press. Both of these editions carry a wealth of introductory material (hundreds of pages, in fact) along with helpful notes and other material. Both use the New American Bible translation, which was produced and revised by American Catholic scholars.

Not quite a study Bible but containing a good deal of help (the introductory articles are slight but there are ample notes) is the *New Jerusalem Bible.* Get the full edition with the introductions and notes, not the "reader's" edition, which strips out the supplementary material.

With Translations, Older Is Not Necessarily Better

Two seventeenth-century English translations of Scripture continue to be widely read. The King James Version (KJV) is a masterpiece of English poetry and prose, worth reading for its literary quality and influence on the English literary tradition. It is widely read, even today.

The KJV was translated by Protestant scholars at a time when Protestants and Catholics were at loggerheads, and sometimes at sword points, and was not acceptable to Catholics. Consequently, they produced their own translation, called the Douay-Rheims Version. Some Catholics continue to rely on it, partly because it has a greater solemnity and gravity than modern translations.

For various reasons, both the KJV and the Douay translation are out of date.

- Since the seventeenth century scholars have learned much about ancient languages and cultures and have progressed in identifying more accurate copies of the Hebrew, Aramaic, and Greek texts of the Bible. This enables present-day scholars to produce more accurate translations.

- English has changed a great deal since the KJV and Douay translations were made. Numerous words have shifted their meaning. Seventeenth-century English is no longer the best vehicle for conveying meaning to twenty-first-century readers. (How well, for example, do you understand Shakespeare?) As Fr. Peter M.J. Stravinskas writes, "While there may be a certain mystique about archaic language, it does much to obscure the meaning of the text."[2]

- Even where these old translations are reasonably accurate and comprehensible, they make the Bible sound old. But the New Testament writings, and much of the Old Testament, sounded lively and contemporary to the first readers. If the Bible did not sound old-fashioned to its first readers, why should it sound old-fashioned to us when we read it today?

- A further problem with the Douay is that it is a translation of a translation. The translators worked from a Latin version of the Bible, rather than directly from the Hebrew, Aramaic, and Greek texts (although they looked at those also). More than half a century ago, Pope Pius XII established the norm that Catholic translations of the Bible should be made from the original languages in order to reflect its meaning as accurately as possible. The bishops at Vatican II emphasized the importance of "correct translations" produced "principally from the original texts of the sacred books."[3]

There is also a Catholic study Bible designed for young people, the *Catholic Youth Bible,* from St. Mary's Press.

My first, very strong, recommendation, then, is to get a study Bible. My second recommendation is to get a second edition of the Bible, using a different translation. No translation is perfect. Each has its strengths and weaknesses. In many cases you will get a better understanding of a biblical passage by reading it in more than one translation. It is like seeing with two eyes instead of one. St. Augustine observed, "An inspection of various translations frequently makes obscure passages clear." On the other hand, you will sometimes find that different editions offer such different translations of a passage that you are left more puzzled than enlightened. But even such a discrepancy between translations is valuable, for it is a signal that the underlying biblical text is ambiguous or obscure—and, therefore, you should be cautious in interpreting and applying it.

Since your second translation is to be supplementary, it need not be a study Bible but may be an edition without many notes or other helps.

What factors might you take into account in choosing your second Bible? Here are a few considerations:

- *Word-for-word versus thought-for-thought translations.* Translators go in one of two directions. Either they try to enable the reader to see the word choices and grammatical structures of the original as much as possible or they try to recreate the effect of the original.

  The first approach seeks what is called *formal equivalence* (reflecting in the translation the forms of the original sentences). This approach involves translating the original text word for word and phrase for phrase.

  The second approach is called *dynamic equivalence* (reflecting the dynamism, the effect, of the original). This approach translates thought for thought and sentence for sentence, but not word for word (see box below).

Each approach has advantages and disadvantages. A dynamic equivalence translation is easier for meditation and prayer. A formal equivalence translation may be better for study. Where the underlying text is ambiguous or obscure, a formal equivalence translation will reflect the ambiguity or obscurity so that you can get some idea of what it is. By contrast, faced with an ambiguous or obscure passage, a dynamic equivalence translation will settle on one possible interpretation, making it impossible for you to detect that there is something unclear about the original. This makes a word-for-word translation better for study; but, if you already have a study Bible, you might want your second translation to be of the thought-for-thought variety.

"Formal" and "Dynamic" Translations Compared

Here are four translations of Romans 12:1-2. The first two are examples of the formal equivalence, or word-for-word, approach. The last two are examples of dynamic equivalence, or thought-for-thought translation.

I urge you therefore, brothers, by the mercies of God, to offer your bodies as a living sacrifice, holy and pleasing to God, your spiritual worship. Do not conform yourselves to this age but be transformed by the renewal of your mind, that you may discern what is the will of God, what is good and pleasing and perfect.

New American Bible

I appeal to you therefore, brothers and sisters, by the mercies of God, to present your bodies as a living sacrifice, holy and acceptable to God, which is your spiritual worship. Do not be conformed to this world, but be transformed by the renewing of your minds, so that you may discern what is the will of God—what is good and acceptable and perfect.

New Revised Standard Version

I urge you, then, brothers, remembering the mercies of God, to offer your bodies as a living sacrifice, dedicated and acceptable to God; that is the kind of worship for you, as sensible people. Do not model your behavior on the contemporary world, but let the renewing of your minds transform you, so that you may discern for yourselves what is the will of God— what is good and acceptable and mature.

New Jerusalem Bible

Therefore, my brothers, I implore you by God's mercy to offer your very selves to him: a living sacrifice, dedicated and fit for his acceptance, the worship offered by mind and heart. Adapt yourselves no longer to the pattern of this present world, but let your minds be remade and your whole nature thus transformed. Then you will be able to discern the will of God, and to know what is good, acceptable, and perfect.

New English Bible

- *Gender language.* Traditionally, English has allowed masculine pronouns sometimes to refer to both men and women. In recent decades, many people have rejected this approach, feeling that it excludes women or renders them invisible. Others have vigorously defended the traditional approach. There are complex linguistic and cultural arguments on both sides of the issue.

To varying degrees, translations follow either a traditional language approach or an "inclusive language" approach.In choosing between these options, the reader's taste plays a major role. But there are some tradeoffs to consider.

A disadvantage of traditional language translations today is that they tend to be somewhat older and therefore do not benefit from the most recent scholarship. For example, the traditional language Revised Standard Version (RSV) is somewhat older and based on slightly dated scholarship. The New Revised Standard Version (NRSV), which uses inclusive language for human beings, is based on more up-to-date scholarship.

On the other hand, inclusive language translations, in their efforts to avoid using generic masculine pronouns and nouns, resort to strategems that blur the meaning of the biblical texts and obscure connections between the Old and New Testaments.

An example is the NRSV rendering of Hebrews 2:6-8, which quotes Psalm 8:4-6. The Hebrew text of Psalm 8 speaks of "man" and "the son of man," meaning humankind. The letter to the Hebrews interprets these terms in Psalm 8 as references to Christ. The psalm's reference to humankind can be connected with Christ, because in Hebrew and Greek, as in traditional English, the word for "man" may refer both to humankind and to an individual male human being. But the NRSV translates these terms, in both the psalm and in Hebrews, as "human beings" and "mortals." It is not easy to see how the plurals "human beings" and "mortals" in Psalm 8 could be taken as references to the individual man Jesus in Hebrews 2.

• *Paraphrases and other deficient versions.* Paraphrases are renderings that are so loose and move so far from the author's ideas and ways of expressing them that the result can no longer be considered a translation. A leading example of a paraphrase is the *Living Bible.*

My advice about paraphrases: Use them with care. A paraphrase may be useful for getting a feel for a passage in Scripture. But if you really want to understand it, you then need to examine it also in a translation that reflects more faithfully what the biblical authors actually wrote.

To be avoided are translations that distort the meaning of Scripture in order to promote a religious or cultural cause. An example of such distortion is the translation of the Jehovah's Witnesses (New World Translation), which tampers with the first verse of John's Gospel in order to support a theological view held by the Witnesses.

Another example is *The New Testament and Psalms: An Inclusive Version.* The Inclusive Version refuses to call God "Father" or Jesus "Son," with the result that Jesus speaks of himself as "the Child" (John 3:35) and prays in Gethsemane: "Father-Mother, if you are willing, remove this cup from me" (Luke 22:42). This translation also obscures the sexual identity of some of the people Jesus meets. Thus Jesus heals a "person" who is paralyzed (Mark 2:1-12) and a "person" who is deaf (Mark 7:31-37). In this translation, the Church is no longer the bride of Christ (Ephesians 5:25-32; Revelation 21:2).

Finally, I recommend that you avoid abridgements, such as the *Reader's Digest Bible.*

Recent English Translations of the Bible

Word-for-word, formal equivalence translations

Revised Standard Version
New Revised Standard Version
New American Bible
New International Version
New American Standard Bible
New Jewish Version

Thought-for-thought, dynamic equivalence translations

Jerusalem Bible
New Jerusalem Bible
New English Bible
Revised English Bible
Today's English Version (Good News Bible)
Contemporary English Version

Learn Your Way Around

Once you have a Bible, you need to find your way around in it.

For many centuries, editions of the Bible have employed a numbered system of longer and shorter divisions to facilitate locating and identifying texts. This system divides the biblical books into short numbered sections called chapters, which may be a page or two in length. Chapters are subdivided into numbered verses, containing a sentence or two (not only the poetry but also the prose is divided into "verses"). The division into numbered chapters and verses was not worked out until the Middle Ages; it is not part of the inspired text.

Unfortunately, for various reasons there are small discrepancies between editions in the divisions and the numberings. Thus, if you are looking for a particular chapter and verse, depending on the edition, you may have to look backward or forward a verse or two to find what you are seeking. In the Book of Psalms, the numbering systems diverge by as much as an entire psalm.

In citing biblical texts it is common to abbreviate the names of the biblical books and to use a shorthand method of referring to the chapter and verse. Unfortunately, there is more than one system of abbreviation and more than one approach to representing the chapter and verse numbers. For example, the first verse of the twelfth chapter of Genesis might be cited as Gen 12:1, Gen 12.1, Gen xii 1, or Gen 12,1. Genesis may be abbreviated Gn.

Not only the abbreviation systems but also the names of some of the biblical books vary. For example, the book called in some versions the Song of Songs is elsewhere called the Song of Solomon or the Canticle of Canticles. Ecclesiastes is sometimes called Qoheleth. Ecclesiasticus is sometimes called Sirach. The last book of the Bible is sometimes called the Apocalypse, sometimes Revelation (not, as it is sometimes mistakenly called, Revelations).

These are relatively minor problems. It should take just a few minutes for you to determine how the version you are using handles titles, abbreviations, and citations of chapter and verse. As a starting point, check the table of contents or the list of books and abbreviations at the front of your Bible. While you are looking at the table of contents, you might also compare the order of the Old Testament books to the list on page 14. Some versions, unlike the list on page 14, gather together the material accepted by Catholics but not by Protestants in a separate section either between the Old and New Testaments or after the New Testament.

It pays to get acquainted with the introductions, notes, maps, and other helps in your Bible. Introductory articles usually contain material about the date, authorship, literary form, and setting of the book. The preceding chapters on how the Bible came to be and how to interpret it should help you see how such information can aid in understanding what the biblical books mean.

Depending on the layout of your version, a study Bible may have as many as three sets of notes accompanying the biblical text, at the foot of the page or in the margins.

One set of notes may give information about the text or translation. For instance, in the RSV after Psalm 85:8, which is rendered "to those who turn to him in their hearts," there is this note: "Gk: Heb *but let them not turn back to folly.*" This tells us that the RSV translators followed a Greek version of the psalm and supplies the meaning of the Hebrew text that they did not follow.

A second set of notes may contain cross-references. These will help you see connections between various passages in Scripture. Many cross-references accompanying the Old Testament will point to passages in the New Testament that speak of Jesus and Christian life. For example, cross-references accompanying Psalm 2 will lead you to the several quotations of this prayer in the New Testament. Thus cross-references are useful for reading the parts of the Bible in light of the whole, that is, in light of Christ.

A third set of notes—often the longest of the three—may offer background information, explanations, and other comments.

Develop a Reading Plan

Although the whole Bible is God's word, not every part of it is equally important. The Gospels are central. The other parts are subordinate to them. Thus we are not obliged to devote equal attention to every biblical book. Indeed, we should focus our attention on those that are most important. This means a focus on the New Testament, especially the Gospels.

A related consideration is that not every part of the Bible is equally interesting or accessible to us. This is to be expected. If you find portions of the Bible hard going, skip them with a clear conscience. Come back at a later date, after you have explored biblical books that are more congenial to you.

Where to begin? My advice is to begin wherever you like. Some experts criticize the begin-at-the-beginning approach, because many first-time Bible readers who start with Genesis get bogged down in Exodus and give up. But there are readers who feel uncomfortable beginning a book anywhere except the beginning and who are not deterred by stretches of dry material. Some people advise beginners to start with the Gospel of Luke or with Luke's companion volume, the Acts of the Apostles. Certainly either book makes an excellent starting point, but there are many others.

I suggest, however, that once you select a biblical book, you read it in its entirety. (Exceptions would be very long books, such as Psalms and Isaiah.) Only by reading a biblical book all the way through can you get its overall message and see how the parts fit into the whole.

I also suggest alternating between New Testament and Old Testament books. If you alternate this way, you will complete your reading of the New Testament first, because there are fewer books in the New Testament. Then, while you continue reading Old Testament books for the first time, you can go back and read the New Testament books a second time.

If you stick with your reading, you will gradually get used to the Bible's atmosphere, background, and themes. As when you move to another part of the country or go to live abroad, the strange becomes familiar little by little. If you stay long enough, you begin to feel at home.

Keep on Learning

Cultivate a learner's attitude. Be on the lookout for talks, courses, TV programs, videos, books, magazine articles, and so on that offer background and insights into the Bible. Acquire some tools for study or at least get to know where they can be found at a parish or public library. The following are basic tools. For specific recommendations, see the next chapter.

- *A Bible dictionary.* This will give you short articles on words, people, places, events, biblical books, and so on. A good single-volume Bible dictionary is an invaluable companion to reading the Bible.

- *Commentaries.* A single-volume commentary will provide a brief chapter-by-chapter explanation of all the books of the Bible. There are also commentary series, in which an entire volume may be devoted to a single biblical book. Be aware that some commentary series are written at a level that is not helpful for a beginner.

- *Material for reflection and application.* Devotional Bibles, books, periodicals, and pamphlets can aid your discussion and journaling, your reflection and prayer. Somewhere out there are materials that will suit your needs and taste. Seek them out!

- *Catechism of the Catholic Church.* The *Catechism* will help you explore how the subjects you encounter in the Bible have developed in the Catholic tradition. Topical and biblical indexes in the back of the Catechism aid in discovering connections between the Bible and Catholic teaching, sacraments, and more.

- *A Bible atlas.* Most of us like to have a map when we travel. Why not travel through the Bible with some maps at hand?

- *A concordance.* A concordance shows all the passages in the Bible where each word is used. This makes it handy for locating passages when you can remember a word but not the chapter and verse. It is also useful for investigating how various biblical authors dealt with a given person, event, or idea.

Chapter Ten

Where Do I Go From Here?
Resources for Biblical Study,
Reflection, and Prayer

A. Introductions to the Bible

Lawrence Boadt, *Reading the Old Testament* (New York: Paulist, 1985).

Dom Celestin Charlier, *The Christian Approach to the Bible,* John M.T. Barton, trans. (New York: Paulist, 1967).

Michael Duggan, *The Consuming Fire: A Christian Introduction to the Old Testament* (San Francisco: Ignatius, 1991).

Jerome Kodell, O.S.B., *The Catholic Bible Study Handbook,* revised edition (Ann Arbor, Mich.: Servant, 2001).

George Martin, *Reading Scripture As the Word of God: Practical Approaches and Attitudes,* revised fourth edition (Ann Arbor, Mich.: Servant, 1998).

George E. Mendenhall, edited by Gary A. Herion, *Ancient Israel's Faith and History: An Introduction to the Bible in Context* (Louisville: Westminster John Knox, 2001).

Steve Mueller, *The Seeker's Guide to Reading the Bible: A Catholic View* (Chicago: Loyola, 1999).

Pheme Perkins, *Reading the New Testament* (New York: Paulist, 1988).

John Rogerson, *An Introduction to the Bible* (New York: Penguin Putnam, 1999).

Arthur E. Zannoni, *A Beginner's Guide to the New Testament* (Allen, Texas: Thomas More, 2002); *A Beginner's Guide to the Old Testament* (Allen, Texas: Thomas More, 2003).

B. Catholic Church Documents

Austin P. Flannery, O.P., ed., *Vatican Council II: The Conciliar and Post Conciliar Documents* (Grand Rapids, Mich.: William B. Eerdmans Publishing. 1984). This book contains the *Dogmatic Constitution on Divine Revelation.*

Joseph A. Fitzmyer, S.J., *The Biblical Commission's Document, "The Interpretation of the Bible in the Church": Text and Commentary* (Rome: Editrice Pontificio Istituto Biblico, 1995). This book contains the Pontifical Biblical Commission's 1993 statement, *The Interpretation of the Bible in the Church,* along with statements by Pope John Paul II and Cardinal Joseph Ratzinger on biblical interpretation, and a commentary by Joseph Fitzmyer. The text of *The Interpretation of the Bible in the Church,* by the Pontifical Biblical Commission, with the comments by the Pope and Cardinal Ratzinger, but without the commentary by Father Fitzmyer, is available from the United States Catholic Conference, in Washington, D.C.

Catechism of the Catholic Church, revised edition (Washington, D.C.: United States Catholic Conference—Libreria Editrice Vaticana, 2000).

C. Tools for Biblical Study

1. Catholic Study Bibles

Jean Marie Hiesberger and others, editors, *The Catholic Bible: Personal Study Edition* (New York: Oxford University, 1997).

Donald Senior, C.P., and others, editors, *The Catholic Study Bible* (New York: Oxford University, 1990).

Eduardo Arnouil and others, editors, *The Catholic Youth Study Bible* (Winona, Minn.: St. Mary's Press, 2000).

2. Dictionaries and Other One-Volume Companions to the Bible

Paul J. Achtemeier and others, eds., *The HarperCollins Bible Dictionary, revised edition* (San Francisco: HarperCollins, 1996).

David Noel Freedman and others, eds., *Eerdmans Dictionary of the Bible* (Grand Rapids, Mich.: William B. Eerdmans Publishing, 2000).

Bruce M. Metzger and Michael D. Coogan, eds., *The Oxford Companion to the Bible* (New York: Oxford University, 1993).

Carroll Stuhlmueller, C.P., ed., *The Collegeville Pastoral Dictionary of Biblical Theology* (Collegeville, Minn.: Liturgical Press, 1996).

3. Atlas

James B. Pritchard, *The HarperCollins Concise Atlas of the Bible* (San Francisco: HarperCollins, 1991).

4. Concordances

Each concordance is keyed to a particular translation. The following concordances are keyed to the New Revised Standard Version:

NRSV Exhaustive Concordance (Nashville, Tenn.: Thomas Nelson Publishers, 1991).

The NRSV Concordance Unabridged (Grand Rapids, Mich.: Zondervan, 1991).

5. One-Volume Commentaries on the Entire Catholic Bible

Dianne Bergant and Robert J. Karris, O.F.M., eds., *The Collegeville Bible Commentary* (Collegeville, Minn.: Liturgical Press, 1989).

Raymond E. Brown, S.S., Joseph A. Fitzmyer, S.J., and Roland E. Murphy, O.Carm., eds., *The New Jerome Biblical Commentary* (Englewood Cliffs, N.J.: Prentice Hall, 1990).

William R. Farmer and others, eds., *The International Bible Commentary: A Catholic and Ecumenical Commentary for the Twenty-First Century* (Collegeville, Minn.: Liturgical Press, 1998).

James L. Mays and others, eds., *The HarperCollins Bible Commentary*, revised edition (San Francisco: HarperCollins, 2000).

6. Other Commentary Series

Sacra Pagina Series. The Liturgical Press.

Spiritual Commentaries Series. New City Press.

7. Commentaries by Church Fathers

Ancient Christian Commentary on Scripture. Selections from Church Fathers on various books of the Bible. InterVarsity Press.

The following series of books contain volumes by Church Fathers on Scripture along with other patristic works:

The Fathers of the Church Series. Among this series' patristic biblical commentaries is the commentary of St. John Chrysostom on Genesis. Catholic University Press.

Ancient Christian Writers Series. Among this series' patristic biblical commentaries are the commentaries of St. Augustine on the Psalms and on the Sermon on the Mount. Paulist Press.

Some of the biblical homilies of St. Chrysostom have also been published by St. Vladimir's Seminary Press.

8. Materials for Discussion, Reflection, and Meditation

"6 Weeks with the Bible" books. Twenty short discussion guides on Old and New Testament books. Loyola Press.

Little Rock Scripture Study Program. Extensive printed, video, and audio materials, with leadership support services, for group Scripture study. Liturgical Press.

Michael Casey, *Sacred Reading: The Ancient Art of Lectio Divina* (Liguori, 1996).

9. Periodicals

God's Word Today Magazine. Explores the Bible book by book and by themes; for personal study, reflection, and prayer. Bayard Press.

Share the Word Magazine. Follows the lectionary. For discussion and reflection. Paulist National Catholic Evangelization Association.

Living Faith Magazine. Follows the lectionary. For meditation and prayer. Creative Communications for the Parish.

The Word Among Us Magazine. Follows the lectionary. For meditation and prayer.

Scripture from Scratch. Video materials and newsletter. St. Anthony Messenger Press.

The Bible Today. Background and explanatory material about the Bible. Liturgical Press.

10. Other Materials

Saint Augustine, *On Christian Doctrine,* D.W. Robertson, Jr., trans. (Upper Saddle River, N.J.: Prentice Hall, 1958).

Raymond E. Brown, S.S., *Responses to 101 Questions on the Bible* (New York: Paulist, 1990).

George T. Montague, S.M., *Understanding the Bible: A Basic Introduction to Biblical Interpretation* (New York: Paulist, 1997).

John J. Pilch, *Choosing a Bible Translation* (Collegeville, Minn.: Liturgical Press, 2000).

Peter M.J. Stravinskas, *The Catholic Church and the Bible* (San Francisco: Ignatius, 1996).

D. Publishers' Addresses

Bayard Press
God's Word Today Magazine
Subscription Services
P.O. Box 56915
Boulder, CO 80322-6915
(800) 246-7390

Creative Communications for
the Parish
1564 Fencorp Drive
Fenton, MO 63026-2942
(800) 325-9414
livingfaith.com

Eerdmans Publishing Co.
255 Jefferson Ave., SE
Grand Rapids, MI 49503
(800) 253-7521
eerdmans.com

InterVarsity Press
P.O. Box 1400
Downers Grove, IL 60515
(630) 734-4000
gospelcom.net/ivpress

Catholic University of
America Press
The Catholic University of
America
Washington, D.C. 20064
cuapress.cua.edu

HarperCollins Publishers
10 E. 53rd Street
New York, NY 10022
(212) 207-7000
harpercollins.com

Ignatius Press
San Francisco, CA
ignatius.com

Liguori Publications
1 Liguori Drive
Liguori, MO 63057-9999
(800) 325-9521
liguori.org

The Liturgical Press
St. John's Abbey
P.O. Box 7500
Collegeville, MN 56321
(800) 858-5450
litpress.org

Thomas Nelson, Inc.
P.O. Box 141000
Nashville, TN 37214
thomasnelson.com

Oxford University Press
198 Madison Ave.
New York, NY 10016
oup-usa.org

Paulist Press
997 MacArthur Blvd.
Mahwah, NJ 07430
(800) 218-1903
paulistpress.com

St. Anthony Messenger Press
1615 Republic St.
Cincinnati, OH 45210
(800) 488-0488
AmericanCatholic.org

Loyola Press
3441 N. Ashland Ave.
Chicago, IL 60657
(800) 621-1008
loyolapress.com

New City Press
202 Cardinal Road
Hyde Park, NY 12538
(800) 462-5980
newcitypress.com

Paulist National Catholic
Evangelization Association
3031 Fourth St., NE
Washington, D.C. 20017-1102
(202) 832-5022
sharetheword.net

Prentice-Hall
1 Lake Street
Upper Saddle River, NJ 07458
(800) 282-0693
prenhall.com

St. Mary's Press
702 Terrace Heights
Winona, MN 55987-1318
(800) 533-8095
smp.org

St. Vladimir's Seminary
Press
575 Scarsdale Road
Crestwood, NY 10707
(914) 961-2203
svots.edu/svs-press

Servant Publications
P.O. Box 8617
Ann Arbor, MI 48107
(800) 458-8505
servantpub.com

The Word Among Us
9639 Doctor Perry Road, #126N
Ijamsville, MD 21754
(800) 775-9673
wau.org

Zondervan
5300 Patterson SE
Grand Rapids, MI 49530
zondervan.com

Notes

For books cited here by title only, see chapter ten for full bibliographic data.

Translations of the Second Vatican Council documents are from one
of three sources:

1. Walter M. Abbott, S.J., editor and others, *The Documents of
   Vatican II* (New York: America Press, 1966).
2. Austin Flannery, O.P., editor, *Vatican Council II: The Conciliar and
   Post Connciliar* Documents, revised edition (Grand Rapids, Mich.:
   Eerdmans, 1988).
3. The author of this book.

Four
Did It Really Happen?

1. *Ancient Israel's Faith and History,* 44.
2. "A Response of the Biblical Commission" to Cardinal E.C. Suhard,
   16 January 1948, in *Rome and the Study of Scripture* (St. Meinrad,
   Ind.: Abbey Press, 1964), 152–53.
3. Author's translation.
4. Abbott translation.

Five
Whose Words Are These?

1. *The Catholic Bible Study Handbook*, 5.
2. *The Christian Approach to the Bible*, 210.
3. *Dogmatic Constitution on Divine Revelation* (11), author's translation.
4. *The Catholic Bible Study Handbook*, 6.
5. Abbott translation.
6. *The Catholic Bible Study Handbook*, 9.

Six
Whose Book Is This?

1. *Dogmatic Constitution on the Church* (1), Flannery translation.
2. Abbott translation.
3. *The Interpretation of the Bible in the Church*, III, B, 1.
4. We are speaking here about the formation of the New Testament. The early Christians did not have to decide the contents of the Old Testament. They simply continued to use the Scriptures of Israel according to the ancient Greek translation, called the Septuagint. Later, however, questions arose about the particular books and parts of books that belonged in the Old Testament, since the Septuagint contained both varying numbers of books and more books than were in the Hebrew collection. See page 85–87, "Why Are the Catholic and Protestant Bibles Different?"
5. *The Catholic Bible Study Handbook*, 17.
6. *The Christian Approach to the Bible*, 236.
7. *Dogmatic Constitution on Divine Revelation* (24).
8. *Dogmatic Constitution on Divine Revelation* (10), author's translation.
9. *Reading Scripture As the Word of God*, 156.

Seven
How Do We Know What It Means?

1. *Dogmatic Constitution on Divine Revelation* (13), author's translation.
2. *Dogmatic Constitution on Divine Revelation* (11), Flannery translation.
3. *Dogmatic Constitution on Divine Revelation* (12), author's translation.
4. *Dogmatic Constitution on Divine Revelation* (11), Flannery translation.
5. John Paul II, "Address on the Interpretation of the Bible in the Church," section 13. in *Interpretation of the Bible in the Church.*
6. Abbott translation.
7. *The Interpretation of the Bible in the Church,* Flannery.
8. John Paul II, "Address," section 8.
9. *Divino Afflante Spiritu* (47).
10. Quoted in *The Interpretation of the Bible in the Church,* "Address," section 5.
11. *The Interpretation of the Bible in the Church,* II, B, 2, b.
12. *The Christian Approach to the Bible,* 268.
13. *Divino Afflante Spiritu* (27).
14. *The Christian Approach to the Bible,* 271.

Eight
How Can It Speak to Me?

1. Author's translation.
2. *Reading Scripture As the Word of God,* 16.
3. *Responses to 101 Questions on the Bible,* 23.
4. *The Seeker's Guide to Reading the Bible,* 187.
5. *The Seeker's Guide to Reading the Bible,* 21.
6. *The Interpretation of the Bible in the Church,* II, A, 2.

7. *Responses to 101 Questions on the Bible,* 28.
8. Henri Nouwen wrote a thought-provoking book on his response to this parable as it was depicted by Rembrandt, entitled *The Return of the Prodigal Son* (New York: Doubleday, 1992).
9. *Dogmatic Constitution on Divine Revelation* (21, 25), author's translation.

Nine
Where Do I Start?

1. *Dogmatic Constitution on Divine Revelation* (25), author's translation.
2. *The Catholic Church and the Bible,* 29.
3. *Dogmatic Constitution on Divine Revelation* (22), author's translation.

Index

General Index

Scripture References

OLD TESTAMENT